Yahweh in Africa

Bible and Theology in Africa

Knut Holter
General Editor

Vol. 1

PETER LANG
New York • Washington, D.C./Baltimore • Boston • Bern
Frankfurt am Main • Berlin • Brussels • Vienna • Oxford

Knut Holter

Yahweh in Africa

Essays on Africa
and the Old Testament

PETER LANG
New York • Washington, D.C./Baltimore • Boston • Bern
Frankfurt am Main • Berlin • Brussels • Vienna • Oxford

Library of Congress Cataloging-in-Publication Data

Holter, Knut.
Yahweh in Africa: essays on Africa and the Old Testament / Knut Holter.
p. cm. — (Bible and theology in Africa; vol. 1)
Includes bibliographical references and index.
1. Bible. O.T.—Criticism, interpretation, etc.—Africa, Sub-Saharan.
2. Cushites. 3. Blacks in the Bible. 4. Bible. O.T.—Criticism,
interpretation, etc. I. Title. II. Series.
BS1188.H57   220'.096—dc21   99-054310
ISBN 0-8204-4934-2
ISSN 1525-9846

Die Deutsche Bibliothek-CIP-Einheitsaufnahme

Holter, Knut:
Yahweh in Africa: essays on Africa and the Old Testament / Knut Holter.
–New York; Washington, D.C./Baltimore; Boston; Bern;
Frankfurt am Main; Berlin; Brussels; Vienna; Oxford: Lang.
(Bible and theology in Africa; Vol. 1)
ISBN 0-8204-4934-2

Cover design by Nona Reuter

The paper in this book meets the guidelines for permanence and durability
of the Committee on Production Guidelines for Book Longevity
of the Council of Library Resources.

© 2000 Peter Lang Publishing, Inc., New York

Printed in the United States of America

Table of Contents

Preface   vii
Introduction   1

Part One: The Old Testament in Africa   7

1.   Old Testament Scholarship in Sub-Saharan Africa   9

2.   It's Not Only a Question of Money! African Old
      Testament Scholarship between the Myths and Meanings
      of the South and the Money and Methods of the North   27

3.   The Institutional Context of Old Testament Scholarship in
      Africa   41

4.   Popular and Academic Contexts for Biblical Interpretation
      in Africa   51

5.   Ancient Israel and Modern Nigeria: Some Remarks from
      the Sidelines on the Socio-critical Aspect of Nigerian Old
      Testament Scholarship   61

6.   Relating Africa and the Old Testament on the Polygamy
      Issue   77

      Part Two: Africa in the Old Testament   91

7.   Africa in the Old Testament   93

8.   Should Old Testament Cush Be Rendered 'Africa'?   107

9.   Is Israel Worth More to God than Cush? An Interpretation
      of Amos 9:7   115

      Bibliography   127
      Index of Authors   149
      Index of Subjects   155
      Index of Biblical References   159

Preface

Several colleagues and friends have encouraged me to collect some of my essays on Africa and the Old Testament into a book, as they have pointed out the current need for analysis and reflection on African interpretation of the Old Testament. I have followed their advice, and this essay collection will hopefully lead to further reflection on what it means to interpret the Old Testament in Africa.

I would like to express my gratitude to those institutions and people that have made this book possible. First, to the School of Mission and Theology (Stavanger), the Nansen Foundation and Affiliated Funds (Oslo), and the Non-Fiction Literature Fund (Oslo), for travel grants that have enabled me to present the essays at various conferences, universities and theological seminaries in different parts of Africa. Further, to the Norwegian Research Council (Oslo), for a grant that covers the printing subsidies of the book. Then, to Prof Phil J. Botha (Pretoria), editor of *Old Testament Essays*, and Dr Paul Ellingworth (Aberdeen), editor of *The Bible Translator*, for permission to republish three of the essays. Also, to Prof Musa W. Dube (Gaborone), Prof Gerald O. West (Pietermaritzburg), and the publishing house E.J. Brill (Leiden), for permission to publish two essays forthcoming in their book *The Bible in Africa*. And finally, to Dr Heidi Burns, Senior Acquisitions Editor of

Peter Lang Publishing, Inc. (Baltimore), for her interest and patience during the preparation of this book and the launching of the new series, Bible and Theology in Africa.

Some of the essays have previously been published elsewhere. The texts of these essays have been reprinted without alteration, but the references (footnotes and bibliography) are reworked and standardised for this book.

I dedicate the book to three African colleagues and friends—Aloo Mojola (Dodoma), Victor Zinkuratire (Nairobi) and Louis Jonker (Stellenbosch)—as a token of gratitude for personal and professional fellowship!

Stavanger, November 1999

Knut Holter

Introduction

"You have to admit that these African scholars publish their strange things in very odd places!"

The scene was an international (and by that word is still understood western) Old Testament conference. I had just presented a paper on some aspects of African interpretation of the Old Testament, and I was—I must admit—somewhat flattered when one of the maestros of the guild approached me afterwards. His response to my paper was, however, not that flattering, and it revealed that I faced severe presentational difficulties. I had meant to outline and analyse positively some major lines in African scholarly interpretation of the Old Testament, and I had, quite enthusiastically, advocated the need for closer interaction between western and African scholars. But what this maestro of the international guild of Old Testament scholarship had perceived was something quite different, a survey of rather exotic curios from the margins of the guild.

The present essay collection may face some of the same presentational difficulties: Let me therefore, right from the beginning, emphasise that this collection is not meant as an introduction to some "strange things published at very odd places". It is rather meant to be a contribution to some of the contemporary hermeneutical discussion in Africa: What does it mean to interpret the Old Testament in Africa today? Of course, this hermeneutical discussion is mainly an African enterprise. Still, Africa is no island, neither is African interpretation of the Old Testament, and I am sure that also non-African scholars and scholarly communities would benefit from interacting with their African counterparts and participating in this hermeneutical discussion. Actually, I think it is high time that western Old Testament scholars, who generally take for granted that African colleagues are familiar with their positions and production, allow the influence to go in both directions, and therefore familiarise themselves with some of the contemporary African discussion.

One reason for this is the fact that the numerical—and probably also spiritual—centre of Christianity is drifting southwards. Africa is a major exponent of this development, as sub-Saharan Africa throughout the 20th century has more or less become a Christian continent. This has important consequences for the global distribution of institutionalised theological and biblical studies. Whereas western theological institutions are being closed down (two or three university faculties of theology in western Europe only this year), sub-Saharan Africa experiences a boom with regard to new theological seminaries and university departments of religion and/or theology. And over time this changing global distribution will obviously influence the foci of Old Testament scholarship.

Another reason why western Old Testament scholars should familiarise themselves with the African hermeneutical discussion is that all the politically correct talk about scholarly internationalisation becomes only empty rhetoric if Africa, or for that matter also the rest of the two thirds world, is not included. Those westerners are surely right, who point out that African scholars only to a certain extent can be said to participate in "our" international discussion; they are seldom to be found in "our" international conferences, and they seldom publish their research in "our" international journals and book series. However, this unfortunate lack of interaction at present does not mean that there is no room or potentiality for interaction in the near future. It only reflects the global economic and political tension between the North and the South within which biblical scholarship also has to work. And, rather than accepting this tension fatalistically, biblical scholars ought to do something about it.

This is the context of the essay collection; all nine essays want to participate in the current hermeneutical discussion in Africa. The essays cover a wide range of aspects of the relationship between Africa and the Old Testament. Still, they can roughly be grouped in two. One group, labelled "the Old Testament in Africa", focuses on the African interpretation or portrayal of the Old Testament, whereas the other group, vice versa labelled "Africa in the Old Testament", focuses on the Old Testament interpretation or portrayal of Africa.

There are six essays in the first group. The initial one (1) draws some research historical lines within African scholarly interpretation of the Old Testament.[1] It is here argued that the 1980s represent a breakthrough, with institutionalised research and publication, and a conscious understanding of the special mission of Old Testament scholarship in Africa. The next essay (2) discusses different aspects of the relationship between African Old Testament scholarship and its western counterpart.[2] Then follows two essays that focus on the contexts of biblical interpretation in Africa. The first (3) analyses the strong preference amongst African Old Testament scholars for comparative studies, arguing that this preference not only reflects tendencies in popular interpretation, but that it is also influenced by the educational and research political priorities of early post-independent Africa, and by deficient infrastructures of the universities and theological seminaries.[3] And the other (4) claims that there is a need for interaction and mutual recognition between lay and professional interpreters of the Old Testament.[4] Finally there are two case studies. The first (5) goes into one particular geographical area, analysing some Nigerian interpretation of

---

[1] "Old Testament Scholarship in Sub-Saharan Africa": The essay was originally written to be published in G.O. West & M.W. Dube (eds.), *The Bible in Africa*. Forthcoming, Leiden: Brill, 2000.

[2] "It's Not Only a Question of Money! African Old Testament Scholarship between the Myths and Meanings of the South and the Money and Methods of the North": The essay was read as a paper at the International Conference on Reconciliation and Restitution: An Old Testament Perspective, University of Stellenbosch (South Africa), September 1996, and it is published in *Old Testament Essays* 11 (1998) 240–254.

[3] "The Institutional Context of Old Testament Scholarship in Africa": The essay was read as a paper at the 16th Congress of the International Organisation for the Study of the Old Testament, Oslo (Norway) August 1998, and it is published in *Old Testament Essays* 11 (1998) 452–461.

[4] "Popular and Academic Contexts for Biblical Interpretation in Africa": The essay was read as a paper at the International Workshop on Old and New Testament in Africa: Learning from the past and planning for the future, University of Stellenbosch (South Africa), May 1999.

the Old Testament that relates to the socio-cultural situation in Nigeria.[5] And the other (6) gives a thematic example, analysing how the Old Testament is used in the discussion of the polygamy question.[6]

In the second group there are three essays. The first (7) gives a general survey and analysis of references to African nations and individuals in the Old Testament, with some remarks also on the interpretation history of these texts.[7] The second (8) discusses different perspectives on a modern rendering of the Old Testament references to the ancient African nation of Cush.[8] And finally, there is an essay (9) that gives an interpretation of Amos 9:7, with particular reference to the function and interpretation history of its reference to Cush.[9]

The essay collection, as I pointed out above, is meant to be a contribution to the discussion of what it means to interpret the Old Testament in Africa today. At the same time, however, the essays also reflect my personal journey into a (to me) new landscape of biblical scholarship. One thing is that my studies of African interpretation of the Old Testament have taken me to conferences, universities and theological seminaries in various parts of East-, West- and Southern Africa. Still, more important than this geographical aspect is the hermeneutical aspect of my journey. By studying the relationship between African interpretation of the Old Testament and its interpretative context, I have also learnt something about the relationship between my own Old Testament interpretation and its western

---

[5]   "Ancient Israel and Modern Nigeria: Some Remarks from the Sidelines to the Socio-critical Aspect of Nigerian Old Testament Scholarship". The essay was read as a paper at the Annual Conference of the Nigerian Association for Biblical Studies, Owerri (Nigeria), October 1995.

[6]   "Relating Africa and the Old Testament on the Polygamy Issue": The essay was read as a paper at the 8th Congress of the Panafrican Association of Catholic Exegetes, Ouagadougou (Burkina Faso), July 1997.

[7]   "Africa in the Old Testament": The essay was originally written to be published in G.O. West & M.W. Dube (eds.), *The Bible in Africa*. Forthcoming, Leiden: Brill, 2000.

[8]   "Should Old Testament Cush be Rendered 'Africa'?": The essay is published in *The Bible Translator* 48 (1997) 331–336.

[9]   "Is Israel Worth More to God than Cush? An Interpretation of Amos 9:7": The essay was originally written on the request from an evangelical theological journal. However, in the end the majority of the editorial board of the journal were "uncertain of the theological emphasis of the article", and it was not published.

interpretative context. This has been a gradual process, and, as a result, the reader of this essay collection may find examples of inconsistency between the essays; I said things three or four years ago which I now would not say, as I realise that it too much reflects my western context.

It is a very intriguing aspect of the 20th century, at least from the perspective of biblical interpretation, that not only the centre of Christianity, but also the centre of interpreting the Bible is drifting southwards. One consequence of this, which eventually will be recognisable also in academic circles, is that even the power of defining scholarly interpretative contexts and research political priorities will be drifting southwards. So, some decades into the new century, a new generation of scholars from the South will probably express quite different concepts than those we have been accustomed to of what counts as "strange things" and "odd places" within an Old Testament scholarship that is really international.

The Old Testament in Africa

· 1 ·

Old Testament Scholarship
in Sub-Saharan Africa

Historically and geographically speaking, the African experience of reading the Old Testament (OT) stretches from that of Jewish and Christian communities in the northern part of the continent two millennia ago, and up till that of today's post-apartheid communities in the southern part of the continent. It also stretches from that of Coptic and Ethiopian communities throughout the two millennia, and up till that of today's rapid growth of new reading communities all over the continent. The scholarly approaches to the reception of the OT in Africa therefore include a wide spectrum of fields, stretching not only from historical critical to literary readings, but also from historical studies of how the OT is read in Jewish, patristic, Coptic and Ethiopian sources, to different kinds of contemporary readings, including inculturation, liberation, post-colonial, and post-apartheid readings.

Within this wide spectrum of fields, the present essay will delimit itself geographically to focus on OT scholarship in sub-Saharan Africa. That is, it will attempt to present how the OT is interpreted by scholars attached to universities, theological seminaries and churches in that major part of the continent which is situated between the Maghribian north, including Ethiopia, and the post-apartheid south;[1] still, for the sake of brevity, "Africa" will be used as an abbreviation for sub-Saharan Africa.

The presentation of OT scholarship in Africa will be organised according to chronological and topical issues. From a chronological point of view OT scholarship in Africa will be followed from the past, that is the 1960s and 70s, here characterised as its background, through the present, that is the 1980s and 90s, here characterised as its breakthrough, and, indeed with some reservations, into the future, that is into the 21st century. And then, within each of these three chronological divisions, the presentation will circle around two sets of topics, the institutional context of OT scholarship in Africa and its thematic orientation.

The past: 1960s and 70s

The first of the three chronological parts, here characterised as the past or background of OT scholarship in Africa, includes the 1960s and 70s. It is, of course, possible to point out examples of OT scholarship in Africa also prior to the 1960s; a number of theological seminaries gave courses in OT studies based on traditional western approaches, often, however, with an open attitude towards the relationship between the OT and the African context.[2] Also, some few African theologians pointed out the possibilities of a more specific African reading of the OT.[3] Still, the political and ecclesiastical independence of the 1960s, together with a rapid growth of theological seminaries and university departments of religion throughout the continent, and also a sudden wave of publications on Africa and the OT, makes it natural to start this survey with the 1960s.

In 1960, at the dawn of independence, Africa had only six universities,[4] but throughout the 1960s and 70s the number increased

---

1   Cf. K. Holter, *Tropical Africa and the Old Testament* (1996) 13–14.

2   Cf. M.S. Bates, *Survey of the training of the ministry in Africa* (1954) 59–61.

3   One example is J.-C. Bajeux, "Mentalité noire et mentalité biblique", A. Abble & al. (eds.), *Des prêtres noirs s'interrogent* (1956) 57–82.

4   For a survey, cf. J.K. Marah, *Pan-African education* (1989) 148–150.

rapidly. The same was the case with the number of theological seminaries.[5] In this period of post-independence the mission of the universities was seen as part of the efforts of national development; politically, economically, and obviously also culturally.[6] In the humanities this led to a focus on African culture and languages, and the departments of religious studies followed this up with research and teaching programmes on African traditional religion.[7] Also with regard to OT studies this focus on African culture was reflected; here as an emphasising of inculturation hermeneutical approaches, that is approaches where the relationship between the texts of the OT and the context of Africa were being elaborated.[8] As a result, a rapidly growing number of studies comparing religio- and socio-cultural parallels between Africa and the OT were published.

A glimpse into this period can be found in an article by Edward G. Newing, who in the late 1960s made a thorough survey of how OT studies were conducted in universities and theological seminaries throughout Eastern and Central Africa; 37 institutions received a questionnaire, 23 answered.[9] Newing found that most institutions exposed their students to some use of the higher critical approaches developed in western OT scholarship; still, only three offered courses in biblical Hebrew. Not surprisingly, Newing was also able to draw parallels to the situation in the West with regard to programmes and textbooks. However, he was very critical of what he found; especially he was sceptical about a rather rigid system of external examinations. As an attempt to improve the situation, he proposed a new four-year college curriculum where courses in OT isagogics, exegesis and theology were related to courses in other theological disciplines, and where questions of relevance were especially addressed. Additional electives in biblical

---

5   Cf. D. Tutu, "Survey of theological institutions in Africa today", *All-Africa Conference of Churches Bulletin* 9 (1976) 7–27.

6   For an introduction, cf. J.F. Ade Ajayi & al., *The African experience with higher education* (1996) 74–143.

7   Cf. J. Platvoet, "The institutional environment of the study of religions in Africa south of the Sahara", M. Pye (ed.), *Marburg revisited* (1989) 107–126.

8   Cf. S. Abogunrin, "Biblical research in Africa", *Africa Journal of Biblical Studies* 1/I (1986) 12–16.

9   E.G. Newing, "A study of Old Testament curricula in Eastern and Central Africa", *Africa Theological Journal* 3 (1970) 80–98.

Hebrew and OT exegesis and hermeneutics were then to be offered for those having the ability to go on to further studies.

To go on to higher degrees in the field of OT, at least in the sense of doing postgraduate studies, meant in most cases in the 1960s and 70s to go to Europe or the USA. A growing number of Africans got their Master's in OT studies from western institutions throughout these two decades, and, eventually, some few also got their doctorates, mainly from Rome,[10] but eventually also from other places in Europe or USA.[11] These first Africans to get doctorates in OT studies were pioneers, and some of them managed to continue their research and participate in the scholarly debate after their return to Africa.[12] Still, as a whole, their influence on the development of OT scholarship in Africa should not be overestimated. Back in Africa, some disappeared into church administration, others drowned in teaching responsibilities, and few of them ever saw the results of their research published.

More influential were those theologians who, in their search for a *theologia africana*, showed a special interest for the OT. This interest, which in particular focused on the so-called African predilection for the OT,[13] was reflected already in the publications of the *Gründer*-generation of African theology, such as for example Kwesi A. Dickson (Ghana), John S. Mbiti (Kenya) and Emmanuel B. Idowu (Nigeria). As a consequence, the late 1960s, and especially the 1970s, experienced a rapid growth in scholarly publications on OT questions, and then in particular publications relating the texts of the OT and the context of

10   Cf. for example B.A. Osuji, *The Hebrew and Igbo concept of religion and sin* (1967); P.D. Akpunonu, *Salvation in Deutero-Isaiah* (1971); L. Monsengwo Pasinya, *La notion de 'nomos' dans le Pentateuque grec* (1973); N.I. Ndiokwere, *Prophecy and revolution* ([1977] 1981).

11   Cf. for example Y. Tesfai, *This is my resting place* (1975); T.L.J. Mafico, *A study of the Hebrew root* שפט *with reference to Yahweh* (1979).

12   Cf. for example L. Monsengwo Pasinya, "Isaïe xix 16–25 et universalisme dans la LXX", J.A. Emerton (ed.), *Congress volume: Salamanca 1983* (1985) 192–207; *idem*, "Le cadre littéraire de Genèse 1", *Biblica* 57 (1976) 225–241; T.L.J. Mafico, "The Old Testament and effective evangelism Africa", *International Review of Mission* 75 (1986) 400–409; *idem*, "The divine compound name יהוה אלהים and Israel's monotheistic polytheism", *Journal of Northwest Semitic Languages* 22/I (1996) 155–173.

13   Cf. K.A. Dickson, "The Old Testament and African Theology", *Ghana Bulletin of Theology* 4 (1973) 31–41.

Africa. An important factor contributing to this development was the launching of several theological journals; of special importance here, as they from the beginning published articles related to the OT, were *Orita* (1967, Nigeria) and *Africa Theological Journal* (1968, Tanzania).

Thematically there was a close relationship between the dissertations written in western institutions and the articles published in Africa, as both very often circled around the relationship between Africa and the OT. Among the dissertations, comparisons were made on different kinds of religio-cultural phenomena; for example, Oko F. Ugwueze (Nigeria) wrote on proverbs, Nathanael I. Ndiokwere (Nigeria) on prophetism, John Onaiyekan (Nigeria) on priesthood, and Buame J.B. Bediaku (Togo) on penitence.[14] And among the articles similar comparisons were made; for example, Samuel G. Kibicho (Kenya) wrote on concepts of God, Bonganjalo Goba (South Africa) on corporate personality, Francis F.K. Abotchie (Ghana) on rites of passage, and Daniel E. Mondeh (Ghana) on sacrifice.[15]

Similar themes were also discussed at three international conferences which took place in the 1970s, conferences that especially focused on biblical scholarship vis-à-vis Africa. These conferences meant a lot to African scholars working with the OT; not least they meant possibilities to interact with fellow African colleagues. The first was "The Jerusalem congress on Black Africa and the Bible" in 1972,[16] where a number of African scholars met Jewish colleagues, mainly from

---

[14] Cf. O.F. Ugwueze, *Igbo proverbs and biblical proverbs* (1976); N.I. Ndiokwere, *Prophecy and revolution* ([1977] 1981); J. Onaiyekan, *The priesthood in pre-monarchial ancient Israel and among the Owe-Yoruba of Kabba* (1976); B.J.B. Bediaku, *Etude comparé de la célébration pénitentielle dans l'ancient testament et chez le peuple Ewe du Togo* (1978).

[15] Cf. S.G. Kibicho, "The interaction of the traditional Kikuyu concept of God with the biblical concept", *Cahiers des Religions Africaines* 2 (1968) 223–238; B. Goba, "Corporate personality: Ancient Israel and Africa", B. More (ed.), *Black Theology* (1973) 65–73; F.F.K. Abotchie, "Rites of passage and socio-cultural organization in African culture and Judaism", F. von Hammerstein (ed.), *Christian-Jewish relations* (1978) 82–89; D.E. Mondeh, "Sacrifice in Jewish and African traditions", F. von Hammerstein (ed.), *Christian-Jewish relations* (1978) 76–81.

[16] The papers of the conference are found in E. Mveng & R.Z. Werblowsky (eds.), *The Jerusalem congress on Black Africa and the Bible* (1972).

Israel, and discussed different topics relating Africa and the OT.[17] Similar topics were also discussed at a conference on "Christian-Jewish relations in ecumenical perspective with special emphasis on Africa" in 1977,[18] this also taking place in Jerusalem.[19] And a third was the conference in Kinshasa in 1978 on "Christianisme et identité africaine",[20] initiated by the Pan-African Association of Catholic Exegetes.[21]

The growing interest in the relationship between Africa and the OT called for a more systematic analysis of the underlying hermeneutical and methodological questions; this enterprise was primarily undertaken by Mbiti and Dickson. Mbiti described the central role played by the Bible, and then not least by the OT, in African Christianity. He pointed out that this especially concerned the African Instituted Churches, but that it, to some degree, also concerned African theology and Christianity in general.[22] Dickson instead focused on similarities and differences between Africa and the OT with regard to world-view, coining the terms continuity and discontinuity between African and OT life and thought,[23] terms which other scholars also started to use in their discussion of the

---

17   Cf. for example E.B. Idowu, "The teaching of the Bible to African students", E. Mweng & R.Z. Werblowsky (eds.), *The Jerusalem congress* (1972) 199–204; E. Mveng, *ibid.*, (1972) 23–39.

18   The papers of the conference are found in F. von Hammerstein (ed.), *Christian-Jewish relations* (1978).

19   Cf. for example F.F.K. Abotchie, "Rites of passage and socio-cultural organization in African culture and Judaism", F. von Hammerstein (ed.), *Christian-Jewish relations* (1978) 82–89; T.L.J. Mafico, "Parallels between Jewish and African religio-cultural lives", *ibid.*, 36–52; J.S. Mbiti, "African Christians and Jewish religious heritage", *ibid.*, 13–19.

20   The papers of the conference are found in D. Atal Sa Angang (ed.), *Christianisme et identité africaine* (1980).

21   Cf. for example J. Nyeme Tese, "Continuite et discontinuite entre l'ancien testament et les religions africain", D. Atal Sa Angang (ed.), *Christianisme et identité africaine* (1980) 83–112; P.M. Renju, "African traditional religions & Old Testament", *ibid.*, 113–118.

22   Cf. J.S. Mbiti, "The biblical basis in present trends of African theology", *Africa Theological Journal* 7/I (1978) 72–85; *idem*, "African Christians and Jewish religious heritage", F. von Hammerstein (ed.), *Christian-Jewish relations* (1978) 13–19; *idem*, *Bible and theology in African Christianity* (1986).

23   Cf. K.A. Dickson, "Continuity and discontinuity between the Old Testament and African life and thought", *Bulletin of African Theology* 1 (1979) 179–193.

relationship between Africa and the OT.[24] In this respect, Dickson very early emphasised the need for a stronger methodological basis in the comparisons between Africa and the OT,[25] rejecting the attempts that previously had been made by some western expatriates[26] at explaining the affinities between the two as due to historical interaction.[27]

Summing up, the 1960s and 70s showed a growing interest in scholarly studies of the OT. While one can hardly talk about an African OT scholarship as such, due to the lack of structures within the continent for research and publication, still, the efforts put into developing theological seminaries and university departments of religion, together with a growing interest in studies of the relationship between Africa and the OT, provide an important background for what was to become African OT scholarship.

The present: 1980s and 90s

Let us now leave the past, that is the 1960s and 70s, and proceed to the present, that is the 1980s and 90s, also here focusing on the institutional context and thematic orientation of OT scholarship in Africa.

The institutional context of OT scholarship in Africa throughout the 1980s and 90s is characterised by two closely related aspects; a growth in the number of Africans doing postgraduate studies in the OT, and a growth in publications on the OT. At present, towards the end of these two decades, many university departments of religion and several theological seminaries have staff members with doctorates in OT studies. Still, much of the training continues to take place in Europe or North America. The connection between Africa and the West in this respect often follows ecclesiastical lines (Catholics: Rome; Evangelicals: USA), but to some degree it also follows historical and political lines (colonial:

---

24 Cf. for example P.M. Renju, "African traditional religions & Old Testament", D. Atal Sa Angang (ed.), *Christianisme et identité africaine* (1980) 113–118.

25 K.A. Dickson, "African traditional religions and the Bible", E. Mveng & R.Z. Werblowsky (eds.), *The Jerusalem congress* (1972) 155–166.

26 See especially J.J. Williams, *Hebrewisms of West Africa* (1930).

27 K.A. Dickson, "'Hebrewisms of West Africa'", *Legon Journal of Humanities* 1 (1974) 23–34; for an alternative view, cf. D.N. Wambutda, "Hebrewisms of West Africa", *Ogbomoso Journal of Theology* 2 (1987) 33–41.

Great Britain, France and Belgium; neo-colonial: USA). However, it is
increasingly being experienced as a problem that the training is given in
a context that both culturally and scholarly is non-African. One result of
this is that questions emerging from cultural and social concerns in
Africa only to some extent are allowed into the interpretation of the OT.
As a consequence, there is a gap between the needs of ordinary African
Christians for modes of reading the OT, and the modes provided by
scholars trained in the western tradition of biblical scholarship.[28]
Another result of the location of the training outside Africa is a feeling,
at least in some cases, of inferiority vis-à-vis the massive western
tradition. This might eventually lead some scholars to neglect their
African context, and instead see "[...] themselves as ambassadors of
Cambridge, Oxford, [the] Tübingen school etc."[29]

As a response to this, several African universities have throughout
the 1980s and 90s developed programmes for postgraduate studies in the
OT; mainly at Master's level, but in some cases also at Ph.D. level. Even
some of the theological seminaries have developed Master's programmes
in OT studies; of special importance are the two evangelical graduate
schools of theology that were established during the 1980s, one in
Nairobi (Kenya) for anglophone Africa, another in Bangui (Central
African Republic) for francophone Africa. The major force in the
development of programmes for postgraduate studies in the OT is found
in Nigeria, whose many university departments of religious studies
gained an international reputation as early as in the 1960s. Here, the
universities in Ibadan and Nsukka awarded their first Ph.D.'s in OT
studies in the first half of the 1980s.[30] Eventually, universities in other
parts of Africa have also done the same, for example in Cameroon[31] and
Kenya.[32]

---

28 Cf. J.S. Ukpong, "Rereading the Bible with African eyes", *Journal of Theology for
Southern Africa* 91 (1995) 3–14.

29 S.O. Abogunrin, "Biblical research in Africa", *Africa Journal of Biblical Studies* 1/I
(1986) 13.

30 Cf. G.O. Abe, *Covenant in the Old Testament* (1983); G.L. Lasebikan, *Prophecy or
schizophrenia?* (1983); D.J.I. Ebo, "*O that Jacob would survive*" (1985).

31 Cf. G. Gakindi, *La benediction aaronique et la b^{e}rakah de l'ancien testament*
(1992).

32 Cf. S. Gitau, *African and biblical understanding of the environment* (1996).

Closely related to the growth in numbers throughout the 1980s and 90s of Africans doing postgraduate studies in the OT is the remarkable growth in scholarly publications on the OT throughout the same two decades. The publications are of varying character and different genres. The most influential genre is probably represented by the articles, published in an increasing number of African scholarly journals. Of great importance here was that the Nigerian Association for Biblical Studies in 1986 launched the *African Journal of Biblical Studies*, which was the first African journal focusing particularly on biblical research in Africa.[33]

A second genre is represented by published versions of doctoral dissertations. Most dissertations are still not published; some of the ones written in Africa are not even abstracted in international bibliographical tools, and hence difficult to trace. However, a few have been published; for example, Leonidas Kalugila (Tanzania) wrote on the wise king, Nathanael I. Ndiokwere (Nigeria) and Samuel S. Simbandumwe on prophetic movements, and Laurent Naré (Burkina Faso) and Philippe D. Nzambi (Dem. Rep. of Congo) on proverbs.[34]

And then, a third genre is represented by OT commentaries. This classical genre of OT scholarship has actually found surprisingly little attention in Africa; still, at least some commentaries have been published, in most cases commentaries with a devotional profile, but also a few with a more scholarly profile.[35] The best known example of the latter is probably Modupe Oduyoye's (Nigeria) commentary on Genesis 1–11, enthusiastically received as a sign that "the age of African biblical theology has dawned".[36] There have also been some attempts at launching African commentary series. One attempt was made in the late 1960s, when John S. Mbiti proposed that African scholars should write a commentary together. However, he abandoned the idea when he found

---

[33] For a recent report from the editor, cf. G.O. Abe, "African Journal of Biblical Studies", *Newsletter on African Old Testament Scholarship* 3 (1997) 12–13.

[34] L. Kalugila, *The wise king* (1980); N.I. Ndiokwere, *Prophecy and revolution* ([1977] 1981); S.S. Simbandumwe, *A socio-religious and political analysis of the Judeo-Christian concept of prophetism and modern Bakongo and Zulu African prophet movements* (1992); L. Naré, *Proverbes salomoniens et proverbes mossi* (1986); P.D. Nzambi, *Proverbes bibliques et proverbes kongo* (1992).

[35] Cf. J.S. Mbiti, *Bible and theology in African Christianity* (1986) 51–52.

[36] O.O. Obijole, "The age of Agrican [sic] biblical theology has dawned!", *Orita* 18/I (1986) 53–55.

that none of those who had promised to write contributions actually managed to do so.[37] Another attempt was made in the 1970s and 80s, when the West African Association of Theological Institutions initiated a "Bible commentary for Africa project". This project aimed at looking "[...] afresh at the Bible with African insights, relating their interpretation to the African past, the prevailing situations of the churches in Africa and the problems of the various societies in Africa."[38] The co-ordinator of this project was Edward Fasholé-Luke (Sierra Leone), and the project ceased after his death in 1991. A recent project, already in progress, aims to produce a Bible for anglophone African readers. The idea is to use an existing English translation and write introductions to books and chapters, and also footnotes to verses, from the perspective of African cultural and religious traditions as well as social, economic and political realities of present day Africa.[39]

These two aspects of the institutional context of OT scholarship in Africa throughout the 1980s and 90s, that is the increased number in Africans doing postgraduate studies in the OT and the growth in publications, are obviously related to the thematic orientation reflected in their research and publications. Here two aspects should be pointed out.

First, it is clear that the inculturation hermeneutical approaches of the 1960s and 70s continued to play a major role also in the 1980s and 90s, often based on comparative paradigms which related certain ideas or motives in the OT to similar ideas or motives in traditional or contemporary Africa. However, as demonstrated by for example Benjamin A. Ntreh (Ghana), Winston R. Kawale (Malawi), and Justin S. Ukpong (Nigeria), there is now a stronger awareness of the methodological questions that are involved.[40]

This preference for contextual approaches can be seen in the topics chosen for doctoral dissertations; in Africa, where for example George L.

37   Cf. J.S. Mbiti, *Bible and theology in African Christianity* (1986) 60.

38   Cf. E.E. Fasholé-Luke, "Bible commentary for Africa project", *Exchange* 10 (1981) 42–45.

39   Cf. V. Zinkuratire, "The African Bible project", *Newsletter on African Old Testament Scholarship* 4 (1998) 7–9.

40   B.A. Ntreh, "Toward an African biblical hermeneutics", *Africa Theological Journal* 19 (1990) 247–254; W.R. Kawale, "Divergent interpretations of the relationship between some concepts of God in the Old Testament and in African traditional religions", *Old Testament Essays* 8 (1995) 7–30; J.S. Ukpong, "Rereading the Bible with African eyes", *Journal of Theology for Southern Africa* 91 (1995) 3–14.

Lasebikan (Nigeria) wrote on prophecy, Samson Gitau (Kenya) on concepts of the environment, and Madipoane J. Masenya (South Africa) on proverbs,[41] but also in the West, where for example Laurent Naré (Burkina Faso) and Philippe D. Nzambi (Dem. Rep. of Congo) wrote on proverbs, Justin Ukpong (Nigeria) on sacrifice, Philibert Rwehumbiza (Tanzania) on concepts of God, and Samuel Abegunde (Nigeria) on translation methods and philosophy.[42] Still, above all the preference for contextual approaches can be seen in the large number of articles published throughout the 1980s and 90s, largely articles comparing different kinds of religio-cultural phenomena in Africa and the OT.[43] Only a very few examples can be mentioned here; Aloo O. Mojola (Kenya) and Temba L.J. Mafico (Zimbabwe) wrote on the names of God,[44] Philibert Rwehumbiza (Tanzania) and S.G.A. Onibere (Nigeria) on sacrifice,[45] and Gabriel O. Abe (Nigeria) and Ofusu Adutwum (Ghana) on aspects of the institution of matrimony.[46] Moreover, it should here be noted that the contextual approach to the OT is not only found in studies on "the OT in Africa", it is also reflected in different attempts at

---

[41] G.L. Lasebikan, *Prophecy or schizophrenia?* (1983); S. Gitau, *African and biblical understanding of the environment* (1996); M.J. Masenya, *Proverbs 31:10-31 in a South African context* (1996).

[42] L. Naré, *Proverbes salomoniens et proverbes mossi* (1986); P.D. Nzambi, *Proverbes bibliques et proverbes kongo* (1992); J.S. Ukpong, *Sacrifice: African and biblical* (1987); P. Rwehumbiza, *A comparative study between the development of Yahwistic monotheism and the concept of God among the Bantu people south of the Sahara* (1983); S.O. Abegunde, *A philosophy and method of translating the Old Testament into Yoruba* (1985).

[43] For bibliographical surveys, cf. G. LeMarquand, "A bibliography of the Bible in Africa", *Bulletin for Contextual Theology* 2/II (1995) 6–40; K. Holter, *Tropical Africa and the Old Testament* (1996).

[44] A.O. Mojola, "A 'female' god i East Africa", *The Bible Translator* 46 (1995) 229–236; T.M.J. Mafico, "The divine name Yahweh Elohim from an African perspective", *Reading from this place* (1995) 21–32; *idem*, "The divine compound name יהוה אלהים and Israel's monotheistic polytheism", *Journal of Northwest Semitic Languages* 22/I (1996) 155–173.

[45] P. Rwehumbiza, *Patriarchal and Bantu cults compared* (1988); S.G.A. Onibere, "Old Testament sacrifice in African tradition", M. Augustin & K.-D. Schunk (eds.), *'Wünschet Jerusalem Frieden'* (1988) 193–203.

[46] G.O. Abe, "The Jewish and Yoruba social institution of marriage", *Orita* 21 (1989) 3–18; O. Adutwum, "The suspected adulteress", *The Expository Times* 104 (1992/1993) 38–42.

finding "Africa in the OT", that is exegetical analyses of how African peoples and individuals are portrayed by the OT; the contributions by David T. Adamo (Nigeria) are here of special importance.[47]

At the same time, however, it should be emphasised that the 1980s and 90s have seen an increasing focus on more traditional exegetical approaches; in other words, there is now a clear interest in interpreting the OT texts without letting the African context of the interpreter being (at least explicitly!) reflected. In the mid-1980s John S. Mbiti argued that Leonidas Kalugila's dissertation (1980) is "[...] one of the very few 'pure' biblical works by African scholars".[48] A decade later one notices that Kalugila is being accompanied by an increasing number of African colleagues. This tendency is obviously reflected in doctoral dissertations written in a western context (like that of Kalugila); for example, Ofusu Adutwum (Ghana) wrote on the Hebrew root bṯḥ, Victor Zinkuratire (Uganda) on Psalm 47 and the kingship of Yahweh, Benjamin A. Ntreh (Ghana) on the political authority in ancient Israel, and Tewoldemedhin Habtu (Ethiopia/Kenya) on OT wisdom theology.[49] To some extent, however, the same tendency is also reflected in doctor dissertations written in Africa; for example, Gabriel O. Abe (Nigeria) wrote on the covenant, D.J.I. Ebo (Nigeria) on hope in Amos, Gèdèon Gakindi (Rwanda) on the Aaronitic blessing, and Malachy I. Okwueze (Nigeria) on mythology.[50]

Furthermore, the tendency to focus on more traditional exegetical approaches is also reflected in minor studies and articles, where publications throughout the 1980s and 90s reflect a wide spectrum within

---

Cf. most recently D.T. Adamo, *Africa and the Africans in the Old Testament* (1998); cf. also K. Holter, "Should Old Testament Cush be rendered 'Africa'?", *The Bible Translator* 48 (1997) 331–336; M. Høyland, "An African presence in the Old Testament?", *Old Testament Essays* 11 (1998) 50–58.

48 J.S. Mbiti, *Bible and theology in African Christianity* (1986) 49.

49 O. Adutwum, *The root בטח in the Old Testament* (1984); V. Zinkuratire, *The kingship of Yahweh in Israel's history, cult and eschatology* (1987); B.A. Ntreh, *Transmission of political authority in ancient Israel* (1989); T. Habtu, *A taxonomy of approaches of five representative scholars to the nature of wisdom in the Old Testament* (1993).

50 Cf. G.O. Abe, *Covenant in the Old Testament* (1983); G.L. Lasebikan, *Prophecy or schizophrenia?* (1983); D.J.I. Ebo, *'O that Jacob would survive'* (1985); G. Gakindi, *La benediction aaronique et la b^erakah de l'ancien testament* (1992); M.R. Okwueze, *Myth: The Old Testament experience* (1995).

the field of OT research. This includes studies on all kinds of exegetical and theological questions; for example, George L. Lasebikan (Nigeria), D.J.I. Ebo (Nigeria), and Edmond G. Djitangar (Tchad) wrote on prophetism.[51] But it also includes other kinds of approaches; for example, David Alao (Nigeria), J.M. Enomate (Nigeria), and Monday U. Ekpo (Nigeria) made historical and research historical studies,[52] whereas Laurent Monsengwo Pasinya (Dem. Rep. of Congo), Hilary B.P. Mijoga (Malawi), and J.O. Akao (Nigeria) made Septuagint and text historical studies.[53]

These two aspects of the thematic orientation of OT scholarship in Africa throughout the 1980s and 90s are not accidental; rather, they represent a conscious understanding of what it means to do OT scholarship in Africa: the responsibility for doing both historical studies of the text and studies of the encounter between the text and the contemporary context. This twofold mission of OT scholarship in Africa was explicitly expressed in the policy statement in the first issue of *African Journal of Biblical Studies* (1986); it said that the journal wanted to promote biblical research and the study of biblical and related languages, but also to encourage biblical scholars to look afresh at the Bible with an African insight, and relate the interpretation to the life situation in Africa. Similar thoughts have also been expressed throughout the 1980s and 90s by a number of OT scholars; one was Daniel N. Wambutda (Nigeria), who emphasised the necessity of an exegetical basis of African theology,[54] another was Samuel O. Abogunrin (Nigeria),

---

51　G.L. Lasebikan, "Prophets as political activists in the ancient Israelite monarchy", *Orita* 17/I (1985) 51–58; D.J.I Ebo, "Another look at Amos' visions", *Africa Theological Journal* 18/I (1989) 17–27; E.E. Djitangar, "La mission de serviteur de Yahweh", P. Adeso & al. (eds.), *Universalisme et mission dans la bible* (1993) 30–39.

52　D. Alao, "The relevance of the Amarna letters to Hebrew origins", *Orita* 16/II (1984) 87–97; J.M. Enomate, "Ezra the scribe", *African Journal of Biblical Studies* 1/II (1986) 148–159; M.U. Ekpo, "Robertson Smith, the 'higher critics' and the problem of prophecy", *Africa Theological Journal* 14/II (1985) 79–90.

53　L. Monsengwo Pasinya, "Isaïe xix 16–25 et universalisme dans la LXX", J.A. Emerton (ed.), *Congress volume: Salamanca 1983* (1985) 192–207; H.B.P. Mijoga, "Some notes on the Septuagint translation of Isaiah 53", *Africa Theological Journal* 19/I (1990) 85–90; J.O. Akao, "The letter of Aristeas and its worth in biblical studies", *Orita* 22/I (1990) 52–63.

54　Cf. D.N. Wambutda, "Hermeneutics and the search for theologia africana", *Africa Theological Journal* 9/I (1980) 29–39.

who argued that: "We cannot properly contextualize unless we first establish the nature of a text."[55]

Summing up, whereas the past, that is the 1960s and 70s, was characterised as the background of OT scholarship in Africa, the present, that is the 1980s and 90s, can be characterised as its breakthrough. This breakthrough is reflected in its institutional context as well as in its thematic orientation. As for the former, OT scholarship in Africa has throughout these two decades experienced a remarkable growth and deliberate institutionalisation of research and publication. And as for the latter, it has developed a conscious understanding of its mission, focusing on the text as an historical entity as well as the encounter between the text and the context of the contemporary reader.

The future

Finally, after these surveys of the past and present, a few words must also be said about the future; where is OT scholarship in Africa heading at the turn of the millennium? It should be emphasised that the present author, as a non-African, does not want to go into what John S. Mbiti has called the role of western theological engineers, that is to give advice on "[...] how African theology should be done, where it should be done, who should do it, what it should say, *ad infinitum*."[56] The following should therefore not be read as recommendations for the future, but rather as attempts at describing and following some lines that are already present, drawing again on the same two sets of topics as previously, the institutional context and the thematic orientation of OT scholarship in Africa.

The number of universities in Africa has increased from six in 1960 to more than one hundred now towards the end of the 1990s. Still, most of these universities have no postgraduate programmes in OT studies. This also includes universities with theological departments.[57] In the same period the number of theological seminaries and bible schools has

55 Cf. S.O. Abogunrin, "Biblical research in Africa", *African Journal of Biblical Studies* 1/I (1986) 18.

56 J.S. Mbiti, *Bible and theology in African Christianity* (1986) 61.

57 Cf. for example K. Fiedler, "Postgraduate theology degrees in Malawi", *Religion in Malawi* 5 (1995) 37–41.

passed one thousand, with far more of the latter than of the former, and only a very few seminaries have developed postgraduate programmes at Master's level. In other words, within both universities and theological seminaries there is still a lot to do with regard to the development of programmes for postgraduate studies in the OT.

Publication will obviously be a key word in the years ahead. The 1980s and 90s were characterised by a preference for one particular genre within publications, the article in a scholarly journal; this, however, at the cost of other genres. To some extent this will continue, as there is a strong need within the guild of scholars to present the research in the form of brief articles. Still, in the years to come other genres will be of importance. One is the scholarly monograph, usually in the form of a published version of a dissertation. This genre will develop, not only due to the increasing number of doctoral dissertations in OT studies, but also due to the increased number of established researchers attached to universities and seminaries. Commentaries and introductory textbooks represent other, and probably more important genres, as there is a strong need for such books written from an African perspective. To some extent this need has to do with money, as western books, generally speaking, are priced at a level that effectively prevents the average African student (and even scholar) from buying them.[58] Still, more important than the question of money is the question of context. The need for commentaries and textbooks written by African scholars is primarily a need for tools that reflect the context of the African students of the OT. As for the commentary, it represents the classical genre of OT scholarship, since all OT scholarship, one way or another, emerges from the interpretation of the texts. However, since the interpretation of a text to some extent also reflects the cultural, religious, and even political and economic context of the interpreter, there is obviously a need for commentaries that reflect the African context. And as for introductory textbooks, there is a need for African contributions concerning all subdivisions of OT studies, that is books on isagogical and historical as well as theological and hermeneutical questions. With regard to the former, it has been argued that there is a tendency towards "de-africanisation" in the prevailing western textbooks on the history and geography of ancient Israel; that is, a more or less deliberate disregard of

---

58   Cf. K. Holter, "It's not only a question of money!" *Old Testament Essays* 11 (1998) 240–254.

• 2 •

It's Not Only a Question of Money!
African Old Testament Scholarship between the Myths and Meanings of the South and the Money and Methods of the North

When I tell surprised European and North-American colleagues that I am doing some research in African Old Testament (OT) scholarship, I am often asked if there actually *is* such an enterprise as an OT scholarship in Africa.[1] Everyone obviously knows the South African branch of the international guild of OT scholarship, quite recently surveyed and documented by Jurie H. le Roux.[2] However, as pointed out by Ferdinand Deist and others,[3] South African OT scholarship has traditionally been so closely tied up to European and North-American scholarship, that it hardly deserves to be labelled *African*—in any meaningful sense of the word. And hence the surprised question: Is there an OT scholarship in Africa, besides the South African one?

---

[1]   Paper read at the International Conference on Reconciliation and Restitution: An Old Testament Perspective, University of Stellenbosch (South Africa), September 1996.

[2]   J.H. Le Roux, *A story of two ways* (1993).

[3]   F. Deist, "South African Old Testament studies and the future", *Old Testament Essays* 5 (1992) 311–331.

As far as the question of corresponding world-views is concerned, already J.-C. Bajeux, one of the authors behind the epoch-making *Des prêtres noirs s'interrogent* from the mid 1950s, argued that Africans are closer to the Bible, and especially to the OT, than to the theology of Aquinas and the philosophy of Aristotle.[6] Similar thoughts have subsequently been expressed by a number of African scholars; in recent years by, for example, J. Nyeme Tese and Venant Bacinoni, who, in general terms point out aspects of continuity between traditional Africa and the OT, and Emeka Onwurah, who focuses on one particular OT text, the mocking song against the king of Babylon in Isaiah 14, arguing that this text reflects ideas and practices familiar to Africans.[7] Let it also be noted that the relationship between the world-views of traditional Africa and OT Israel in recent years has also attracted several South African OT scholars;[8] of special importance here are the contributions by Jasper Burden.[9]

Far more attention, however, is given to studies expounding the numberless examples of the assumed religio-cultural affinities between OT Israel and traditional Africa. Early attempts at describing and explaining some of these affinities are found in studies by western expatriates. An example from East Africa is Moritz Merker's study of the Maasai (1904), where a number of affinities between the Maasai and OT Israel are pointed out, and said to reflect that the Maasai and OT Israel once constituted one single people.[10] Another example is Joseph J. Williams' study of the so-called "Hebrewisms" in West Africa (1930); he is especially focusing on the Ashanti, and here too are the affinities between these African traditions and those of OT Israel explained as

---

6   J.-C. Bajeux, "Mentalité noire et mentalité biblique", A. Abble & al. (eds.), *Des prêtres noirs s'interrogent* (1956) 57–82.

7   J. Nyeme Tese, "Continuite et discontinuite entre l'Ancien Testament et les religions africaine", D. Atal Sa Angang & al. (eds.), *Christianisme et identite africaine* (1980) 83–112; V. Bacinoni, "Bible et identite africaine", *Theologie africaine* (1989) 241–255; E. Onwurah, "Isaiah 14: Its bearing on African life and thought", *Bible Bhashyam* 13 (1987) 29–41.

8   Cf. for example R. de W. Oosthuizen, "African experience of time", *Old Testament Essays* 6 (1993) 190–204.

9   J.J. Burden, "World-view in interpreting the Old Testament in Africa", *Old Testament Essays* 4 (1986) 95–110; cf. also his "Are Shem and Ham blood brothers?", *Old Testament Essays* 1 (1983) 49–72.

10   M. Merker, *Die Masai* (1904).

reflecting some kind of an historical interaction between the two.[11] These seminal works by western expatriates have clearly influenced African scholars. Especially Williams' book has, for obvious reasons, been met with interest by West African scholars. In an article from the mid 1970s, Kwesi Dickson criticises Williams' methodology and rejects the idea of an historical contact between West Africa and OT Israel. However, Dickson maintains that comparisons between the OT and African life and thought have their value, partly for pedagogical reasons and partly in that they relate to the quest for an African theology.[12] Towards the end of the 1980s Daniel N. Wambutda went in the opposite direction. He praises Williams' methodology as excellent and argues that some sort of interaction in the past is impossible to rule out.[13] During the time between Dickson's and Wambutda's assertions throughout the 1980s, the idea of an historical relationship between ancient Israel and certain West African traditions was also advocated by Modupe Oduyoye, in his commentary on Genesis 1–11,[14] as well as in a large number of articles where different aspects of the assumed affinities between the two are expounded.[15]

Regardless of the methodological hesitation expressed by Dickson and others vis-à-vis the idea of an historical interaction between OT Israel and traditional Africa, the assumed religio-cultural affinities between the two are still considered a major theme within African OT scholarship. And from more phenomenological points of view a large number of studies have investigated certain OT texts and themes—in the light of corresponding African phenomena; such as for example those by

---

[11] J.J. Williams, *Hebrewisms of West Africa* (1930).

[12] K.A. Dickson, "'Hebrewisms of West Africa'", *Legon Journal of Humanities* 1 (1974) 23–34.

[13] D.N. Wambutda, "Hebrewisms of West Africa", *Ogbomoso Journal of Theology* 2 (1987) 33–41.

[14] M. Oduyoye, *The sons of the gods and the daughters of men* (1984). It should be noted that Oduyoye in this book makes no explicit references to Williams' book; however, his debt to Williams is confirmed in his previous article "An African Christian's evaluation of Judaism", F. von Hammerstein (ed.), *Christian-Jewish relations* (1978) 62–66, 64.

[15] M. Oduyoye is the author of no less than ten articles on different aspects of the relationship between the OT and traditional religion in E.A.A. de Adegbola (ed.), *Traditional religion in West Africa* (1983).

similar approach is made by another Nigerian, D. Olubunmo, who uses the OT motive of an ideal king as a model for contemporary Nigerian politics.[26]

Now, it would probably be no exaggeration to say that western OT scholars are rather unfamiliar with this predilection of our African colleagues for comparative studies, not least with the socio-political ones. Nevertheless, such studies are characteristic of African OT scholarship. And hence the next question: what is the relationship between this African OT scholarship—and its western counterpart?

African OT scholarship—and "the money and methods of the North"

Whereas African OT scholarship can be characterised by a *presence* within the social, political, and ecclesiastical context of Africa, it likewise can be characterised by an *absence* within international—that is western—OT scholarship. This marginalisation of African OT scholarship can be recognised at two levels. The first level concerns the scholars themselves. As far as I have personally been able to notice, black African scholars are, generally speaking, absent when the international guild of OT scholars convene in conferences and congresses. Let the congress in Cambridge last year (1995) of the International Organisation for the Study of the Old Testament be used as an example. One should have thought that a congress taking place in the midst of British scholarship and culture would also have had attracted African scholars, but, as far as I could see, amongst several hundred participants from Japan and Korea in the east to California in the west, only one black African was present, Dr. Aloo Mojola, a translation consultant of the Bible Society in Tanzania.[27]

---

26 D.A. Olubunmo, "Israelite concept of ideal king", *African Journal of Biblical Studies* 6/II (1991) 59–67.

27 At the congress Dr. Mojola read a short paper on "Understanding ancient Israelite social structure. Some conceptual confusions: A Bible translator's dilemma"; a revised version is now published as "The 'tribes' of Israel?", *Journal for the Study of the Old Testament* 81 (1998) 15–29. Some of the same ideas had also been presented previously in his article "Translating the term 'tribe' in the Bible—with special reference to African languages", *The Bible Translator* 40 (1989) 208–211.

The second level of this marginalisation of African OT scholarship concerns its scholarly production. African OT scholars certainly publish, but very seldom one finds that they publish their studies in western series and journals. And as few western OT scholars regularly read African journals as for example *Ogbomoso Journal of Theology* or even *African Journal of Biblical Studies*, and further, as few of these journals are being indexed in for example *Old Testament Abstracts* or *Internationale Zeitschriftenschau für Bibelwissenschaft und Grenzgebiete*, the inevitable result is that publications by African OT scholars are often missed by their western colleagues. However, this marginalisation also concerns studies by African OT scholars which are published in the West. One example is Modupe Oduyoye's commentary on Genesis 1–11 from 1984,[28] which, in spite of probably being the African OT commentary which is best known outside Africa, it still is generally ignored in subsequent western scholarship on Genesis 1–11, such as for example in the introductions and commentaries by Gordon Wenham (1987), Donald Gowan (1988), Nahum Sarna (1989), John Rogerson (1991), or John Scullion (1992).[29] Another example is Laurent Naré's monograph from 1986, where he compares the so-called Solomonic collections in Proverbs with proverbs of the Mossi of Burkina Faso;[30] this contribution is ignored even in Friedemann Golka's studies of the relationship between African and OT proverbs.[31]

Let me use two key-words to comment on this western marginalisation of African OT scholarship, the key-words *money* and *methods*. Contrary to, for example, colleagues in the departments of chemistry or physics, OT scholars do not need large laboratories with sophisticated and expensive technological equipment. But what they *do* need, is access to the market place, where current scholarly products are being offered, evaluated and exchanged. And access to this market place, that is scholarly literature, data bases, and to a certain extent also scholarly conferences, is certainly a question of money. When university

---

[28]   M. Oduyoye, *The sons of the gods and the daughters of men* (1984).

[29]   G.J. Wenham, *Genesis 1–15* (1987); D.E. Gowan, *From Eden to Babel* (1988); N.M. Sarna, *Genesis* (1989); J. Rogerson, *Genesis 1–11* (1991); J.J. Scullion, *Genesis* (1992).

[30]   L. Naré, *Proverbes salomoniens et proverbes mossi* (1986).

[31]   F.W. Golka, *The leopard's spots* (1993); this monograph also includes some of his previously published articles on the same topic.

My point is not that a literary approach is better than the historical-critical one, and that the best of all is to let the OT be interpreted by South Africans brought up under the apartheid regime, or West Africans brought up in a traditional village. My point is rather that OT scholarship should be open to all kinds of approaches to the OT, and hence be careful of not defining only certain traditional approaches as "scientific". Such a methodological openness and plurality, I think, is of basic importance to any encounter between western and African OT scholarship.

African OT scholarship—a challenge to western OT scholarship

By now it should be clear that I would very much like to see a closer interaction between African and western OT scholarship. I am certain that both parties will have a lot to learn from each other; but let me here—very briefly—point out two areas where I think the western tradition of OT scholarship would benefit from a closer contact with its African counterpart.

The first area concerns the question of relevance. African scholars are, generally speaking, far more eager than their western colleagues in emphasising that OT scholarship should serve church and society. Now, the question of relevance is certainly alive also in western OT scholarship, as demonstrated by, for example, the renewed interest for OT ethics.[38] Nevertheless, within African OT scholarship the question of relevance is being emphasised almost towards becoming its *raison d'être*. In an article from the mid 1980s on the current state of Biblical studies in Africa, Nlenanya Onwu points out different problems facing church and society in contemporary Africa, arguing that these "[...] should be the core concerns of Africans in biblical studies today."[39] And, likewise, in the first issue of *African Journal of Biblical Studies* in 1986, in a policy article on the task ahead for Biblical research in Africa, Samuel Abogunrin argues that: "Biblical scholars in Africa cannot come to the text in a personal vacuum, but rather with the awareness of the concerns stemming from their cultural background, contemporary

---

[38] Cf. for example E. Otto, *Theologisches Ethik des Alten Testaments* (1994); J.W. Rogerson & al. (eds.), *The Bible in ethics* (1995); D.A. Knight (ed.), *Ethics and politics in the Hebrew Bible* (1995).

[39] N. Onwu, "The current state of biblical studies in Africa", *Journal of Religious Thought* 41 (1985) 46.

situation and responsibility to the Church."[40] I believe African OT
scholars, in their emphasising of the question of relevance, challenge
their western colleagues on a crucial point, the basic definitions of OT
scholarship's what and why. And without listening to these concerns, I
fear that the guild of western OT scholarship might eventually face the
danger of ending up with being of interest to nobody but itself.

A second area where I think the western tradition of OT scholarship
would benefit from a closer contact with Africa, would be to include the
religio- and socio-cultural comparative material Africa has to offer into
its scholarship. Western scholars are of course familiar with some of this
material, for example that of the Nilotic Nuer society. Western scholars
are also familiar with the huge methodological problems attached to any
comparison between the ancient texts of the OT and a society of
contemporary Africa.[41] In spite of this, a sound use of this African
religio- and socio-cultural comparative material will probably prove to
be very fruitful, as it is, for example, demonstrated by Friedemann Golka
in his studies of the relationship between African and OT proverbs.[42] Let
me here add that there is an important ethical aspect linked to a western
use of this African comparative material; it could be called "the palm oil
aspect". Western scholars belong to a context that is accustomed to think
of Africa mainly as a provider of raw materials, such as palm oil, or, in
our case, comparative material for OT scholarship, which then can be
brought to Europe and North America and processed into finished
commodities, such as soap, or, in our case, articles and books.[43] On this
background I should like to emphasise how important it is that western
OT scholars who include African comparative material in their studies,
also include African scholars.

A final word. In the epilogue following his study of South African OT
scholarship in the period 1957–1987, Jurie le Roux expresses a rather
pessimistic view vis-à-vis the future. Having surveyed the efforts put into

---

40 S.O. Abogunrin, "Biblical research in Africa", *African Journal of Biblical Studies* 1
(1986) 14.

41 Cf. for example D. Fiensy, "Using the Nuer culture of Africa in understanding the
Old Testament", *Journal for the Study of the Old Testament* 38 (1987) 73–83.

42 Cf. F.W. Golka, *The leopard's spots* (1993).

43 Cf. C.L. Miller, "Literary studies and African literature", R.H. Bates & al. (eds.),
Africa and the disciplines (1993) 213–231, 227.

obviously demonstrate some affinity with the Old Testament.[4] Still, to some extent the phenomenon is also present within the contexts of Catholic and main stream Protestant churches, and it cannot be brushed away as reflecting supposedly marginal voices only. In different ways, through hymns and sermons, but also through rituals and the visible arts, and, surely, on different levels too, from that of the sermon of the illiterate lay preacher to that of the theological investigation of the university professor, the central role of the Old Testament constitutes an important aspect of African Christianity.

This phenomenon, which is often referred to as "the African predilection for the Old Testament", was described already by Kwesi A. Dickson, John S. Mbiti, and other exponents of the *Gründer*-generation of African theology.[5] They, and also subsequent scholars, have made different attempts at explaining this so-called predilection. One possible explanation, it has been argued, could be the legalism of the early missionaries, another the political appeal of the Old Testament, presumably felt attractive to both colonial and early post-colonial Africa. Even though it should be admitted that this is indeed a complex phenomenon, it is, nevertheless, generally acknowledged that the major explanation of the so-called predilection for the Old Testament is that many Africans experience some sort of a correspondence between their own religio-cultural heritage and what they find in the Old Testament. What missionaries, anthropologists and other expatriates encountering

---

4   For a general introduction to the hermeneutics of African instituted churches, cf. Z. Nthamburi & D. Waruta, "Biblical hermeneutics in African instituted churches", H.W. Kinoti & J.M. Waliggo (eds.), *The Bible in African Christianity* (1997) 40–57. For case studies, cf. for example N. Ndungu, "The Bible in an African independent church", *ibid.* (1997) 58–67; D.C. van Zyl, "Interpretasie van die Ou Testament in Sionistiese kerke", *Nederduitse Gereformeerde Teologiese Tydskrif* 38 (1997) 85–93; H.B.P. Mijoga, "Hermeneutics in African instituted churches in Malawi", *Missionalia* 24 (1996) 358–371; D.C. van Zyl, "In Africa theology is not thought out but danced out", *Old Testament Essays* 8 (1995) 425–438; G.C. Oosthuizen, "Hebraïes-judaïstiese trekke in die onafhanklike kerke (OK) en religieuse bewegings op die swart bevolkung in Suid-Afrika", *Nederduitse Gereformeerde Teologiese Tydskrif* 30 (1989) 333–345.

5   Cf. for example K.A. Dickson, "The Old Testament and African theology", *Ghana Bulletin of Theology* 4 (1973) 31–41; *idem, Theology in Africa* (1984) 141–184; J.S. Mbiti, "The biblical basis in present trends of African theology", *Africa Theological Journal* 7 (1978) 72–85; *idem, Bible and theology in African Christianity* (1986).

traditional Africa have likened with "living in Old Testament times",[6] is also felt by many Africans themselves, at least many of those who have some personal experience with traditional Africa.

This experience of a correspondence between the African religio-cultural heritage and the Old Testament is also reflected in the research of African Old Testament scholars. Up till now, most of them have been trained in Europe or in the United States. However, in recent years an increasing number have received their scholarly training on the African continent, as several university departments of religion or theology and also some few theological seminaries throughout the 1980s and 90s have developed postgraduate programmes that encourage research related to the Old Testament. A large proportion of the research of those trained in Africa, but, actually, also of those Africans trained in the West, focuses on approaches where the Old Testament somehow is read in the light of different kinds of comparative material from traditional Africa. In other words, not only African Christianity in general, but also African Old Testament scholarship is in many ways influenced by the traditional African context.[7]

However, amidst this acknowledgement of the influence of the traditional African context, there is also another but less acknowledged context of African Old Testament scholarship that deserves some attention, namely its institutional context. And hence the question to be posed in this paper: How has the incipient stage of the 1980s and 90s of an Old Testament scholarship in Africa been influenced by the institutional context of those university departments of religion or theology and those theological seminaries that have developed postgraduate programmes encouraging research related to the Old Testament? Let me quite briefly comment on two aspects of this institutional context.

---

6   Cf. E.E. Evans-Pritchard, *Nuer religion* (1970) vii.

7   For a survey, cf. K. Holter, "Old Testament scholarship in sub-Saharan Africa", G.O. West & M.W. Dube (eds.), *The Bible in Africa* (2000); cf. also G.O. West, "On the eve of an African biblical studies", *Journal of Theology for Southern Africa* 99 (1997) 99–115. For bibliographical documentation, cf. G. LeMarquand, "A bibliography of the Bible in Africa", *Bulletin for Contextual Theology in South Africa* 2/2 (1995) 6–40; K. Holter, *Tropical Africa and the Old Testament* (1996).

languages, and those universities which had structures allowing for religious studies focused on African traditional religion.[15]

With regard to Old Testament scholarship this has had two consequences. First, it has led to the quest for a contextualised methodology.[16] When African Old Testament scholarship so strongly focuses on comparative studies, investigating different kinds of religio- and socio-cultural parallels between traditional Africa and the Old Testament, it reflects a deliberate will to present an independent African approach to Old Testament scholarship. A second consequence is the quest for relevance. African Old Testament scholarship concentrates on topics that are experienced as being of relevance to contemporary church and society. In the state universities this is part of a more general demand for a scholarship that contributes to national development. And in the church-related universities and theological seminaries the quest for relevance obviously reflects their primary *raison d'être*, that is to foster a Christian nation—through education and research.

This focus on a contextualised methodology and on the question of relevance is reflected in various ways. Already in the mid 1980s African biblical scholars discussing research political issues argued that these two concerns ought to characterise an africanised biblical scholarship.[17] And a large number of examples show that this was followed up in practice. One illustrative example could be the first chief objectives of the Faculty of Theology, Catholic Higher Institute (now: Catholic University) of Eastern Africa, Nairobi (Kenya), which says that "With special reference to African cultures, CHIEA provides a profound understanding of Christian revelation as found in the Scriptures [...]".[18] Another example could be the policy statement of *African Journal of Biblical Studies*, which says that the journal aims to "Encourage biblical

---

15   For a survey, cf. P. McKenzie, "The history of religions in Africa", M. Pye (ed.), *Marburg revisited* (1989) 99–105.

16   Cf. F.E. Deist, "Biblical interpretation in post-colonial Africa", *Svensk Teologisk Kvartalskrift* 72 (1996) 110–118; J.S. Ukpong, "Rereading the Bible with African eyes", *Journal of Theology for Southern Africa* 91 (1995) 3–14; G.L. Yorke, "Biblical hermeneutics", *Religion & Theology* 2 (1995) 145–158.

17   Cf. N. Onwu, "The current state of biblical studies in Africa", *Journal of Religious Thought* 41 (1985) 35–46; S.O. Abogunrin, "Biblical research in Africa", *African Journal of Biblical Studies* 1/I (1986) 7–24.

18   "CHIEA: The Catholic Higher Institute of Eastern Africa: Faculty of Theology", *African Ecclesiastical Review* 28 (1986) 58–62, 59.

scholars to look afresh at the Bible with an African insight, and relate their interpretation to the past and the prevailing situation in Africa."[19] This journal is published by the Nigerian Association for Biblical Studies, which primarily organises biblical scholars working in state universities in Nigeria. And when these scholars convene to their annual conferences they follow this up, as they always choose themes that relate biblical scholarship to some current socio-political issue.[20]

In a sum, therefore, the education and research policy of African universities and theological seminaries is of major importance for understanding African Old Testament scholarship. First, the almost explosive growth of academic institutions has created a number of structural possibilities for Old Testament scholarship; possibilities which, however, have a somewhat unequal distribution throughout the continent. And secondly, the determined will to contextualise the methodology and to focus on the question of relevance explains some of the focusing on comparative studies. In other words, the institutional context of Old Testament scholarship in Africa has led to an africanised scholarship that lets the traditions and questions of the people of Africa encounter the Old Testament.

Infrastructure and economic resources

The second aspect I would like to point out, of the institutional context of African Old Testament scholarship, concerns its infrastructure and economic resources. It probably comes as no surprise when I say that both universities and theological seminaries in Africa are generally under-funded.[21] The consequences of this are many, but one which is felt particularly badly for the individual scholar, is that it complicates most

---

19 The policy statement can be found in every issue of the journal.

20 Cf. for example "Biblical perspectives of leadership role in nation building" (the conference in Jos, 1991), "Biblical perspectives of ethics and morality in nation building" (Uyo, 1992), and "Biblical principles for moral foundation for the Nigerian society" (Owerri, 1995).

21 For brief surveys presenting some of the economic difficulties, cf. S.O. Atteh, "The crisis in higher education in Africa", *Issue: Quarterly Journal of Opinion* 24 (1996) 36–42; E.S. Etuk, "African universities", *Issue: Quarterly Journal of Opinion* 24 (1996) 43–44.

college and university libraries which at the same time had an average of 78 books per student.[26]

In a sum, therefore, not only the education and research policy of African universities and theological seminaries, but also their infrastructure and economic resources, are important for understanding the institutional context of African Old Testament scholarship. The chronic situation of being under-funded makes it difficult for the individual Old Testament scholar to interact with non-African scholarship, both at a personal level and with regard to scholarly literature. The obvious consequence of this lack of interaction with non-African scholarship, which for all practical purposes is western scholarship, is that the African researcher is left to work with the only material available, that is the African comparative material.

Let me conclude. The 1980s and 90s, which represent the incipient stage of an Old Testament scholarship in Africa, is characterised by a preference for comparative studies that investigate different kinds of religio- and socio-cultural parallels between traditional Africa and the Old Testament. What I have suggested in this paper is that this preference not only reflects the general interest of African Christianity in reading the Old Testament in the light of the traditional African context, but that it also reflects some of the institutional context of Old Testament scholarship in Africa. Positively, it reflects deliberate priorities of institutions promoting a scholarship that focuses on a contextualised or africanised methodology, and that also emphasises the quest for relevance in the African context. Negatively, however, it also reflects unfortunate consequences of the fact that these institutions are constantly under-funded, and particularly their failure to create an infrastructure that makes interaction with non-African scholarship possible.

Taken together these two aspects of the institutional context of African Old Testament scholarship have throughout the 1980s and 90s enforced the already existing interest within African Christianity for relating Old Testament texts to the traditional African context, and in the foreseeable future they will probably continue doing so.

---

[26]   Cf. W.S. Saint, *Universities in Africa* (1992) 7–14.

· 4 ·

Popular and Academic Contexts
for Biblical Interpretation in Africa

There is a famous story that is told in East Africa: "A village woman used to walk around always carrying her Bible. 'Why always the Bible?' her neighbours asked teasingly. 'There are so many other books you can read.' The woman knelt down, held the Bible above her head and said, 'Yes, of course there are many books which I could read. But there is only one book which reads me.'"[1]

The main topic of this session is the relationship between biblical interpretation in Africa and the context of this interpretation. The present paper will then—with the East African village woman in mind—reflect on this topic from two perspectives. First, I will make a brief presentation of two different contexts for biblical interpretation in Africa—that is the popular and academic contexts—and their respective interpretations. And secondly, I will discuss some aspects of the interaction between these two contexts and their interpretations. The

---

[1] Paper read at the International workshop on Old and New Testament in Africa: Learning from the past and planning for the future, University of Stellenbosch (South Africa), May 1999. The East African story is quoted from H.R. Weber, *The Book that reads me* (1995) ix.

Turning to the non-verbal interpretations of the Bible we find the same. In the visible arts the biblical narratives and motives are often given an interpretation that reflects African culture and values,[8] and several studies have pointed out how not least African Instituted Churches let drama, dance, and different kinds of rituals relate the African experience of life and faith to the Bible.[9]

In spite of the research just referred to, I would like to emphasise that a lot remains to be done with regard to analysis of the contextual impact of ordinary people's interpretation of the Bible. With regard to the verbal expressions of this interpretation there is an obvious need for more field studies; the data from Malawi and Nigeria should be related to other regional studies. And with regard to the non-verbal expressions there is—I would argue—a special need for studies of the hermeneutics that is reflected in the various religious rituals that somehow are being related to the Bible. Let me here suggest two areas of research: First, studies of the relationship between (i) rituals that are described in the Bible (mainly Old Testament) and then revived and transferred into contemporary church life,[10] and (ii) rituals which originally belonged to African traditional religion or Islam, and then are taken into the church and legitimised by reference to the Bible (mainly Old Testament).[11] And

---

8   For an example of this, cf. G.O. West, *Contextual Bible study* (1993) 54–59, who argues that the South African artist Azariah Mbatha's woodcut of the Joseph narrative (Genesis 37–50) reflects an interpretation that emphasises central African values.

9   For West Africa, cf. D.T. Adamo "The distinctive use of Psalms in Africa", *Melanesian Journal of Theology* 9 (1993) 94–11; and S. Ademiluka, "The use of therapeutic psalms in inculturating Christianity in Africa", *African Ecclesiastical Review* 37 (1995) 221–227. For East Africa, cf. N. Ndungu, "The Bible in an African independent church", H.W. Kinoti & J.M. Waliggo (eds.), *The Bible in African Christianity* (1997) 58–67. And for Southern Africa, cf. G.C. Oosthuizen, "Hebraïes–judaïstiese trekke in die onafhanklike kerke (OK) en religieuse bewegings op die swart bevolkung in Suid-Afrika", *Nederduitse Gereformeerde Teologiese Tydskrif* 30 (1989) 333–345; D.C. van Zyl, "In Africa theology is not thought out but danced out", *Old Testament Essays* 8 (1995) 425–438; and *idem*, "Interpretasie van die Ou Testament in Sionistiese kerke—'n verkennende studie", *Nederduitse Gereformeerde Teologiese Tydskrif* 38 (1997) 85–93.

10   Cf. the examples in N. Ndungu, "The Bible in an African independent church", H.W. Kinoti & J.M. Waliggo (eds.), *The Bible in African Christianity* (1997) 58–67.

11   Cf. the examples in D.T. Adamo, "The distinctive use of Psalms in Africa", *Melanesian Journal of Theology* 9 (1993) 94–11; and S. Ademiluka, "The use of

secondly, studies of whether—or to what extent—these two sets of rituals (i and ii) are attested also in the historical churches, and not only in the African Instituted Churches, which researchers till now have focused on.[12]

The academic context
Let me then turn to the academic context of biblical interpretation in Africa—that is the context of theological seminaries and university departments of theology or religion. The biblical interpreters one finds in this context are the professional theologians and exegetes. These scholars are in most cases—at least till now—trained in a western context; still, they are to do their interpretation in Africa.[13] Their interpretation of the Bible, as we know it from different kinds of publications, tend to have two areas of focus; one is traditional biblical interpretation as we know it from the non-African guild of biblical scholarship, the other is different kinds of interpretations that somehow try to read the biblical texts in the light of the African experience.

Very little has been done with regard to research on the what's and why's of African biblical scholarship—that is, what African interpreters have focused on in their research, and why they have done so. There are some few preliminary bibliographical surveys,[14] and there are also some

---

therapeutic psalms in inculturating Christianity in Africa", *African Ecclesiastical Review* 37 (1995) 221–227.

12 My impression is that the presence of both sets of rituals is stronger within the historical churches than what is generally acknowledged. Let a couple of examples from Madagascar demonstrate this: Within the Lutheran Church in Madagascar the female leader of the revival movement, Nenilavah, was dressed in an exact copy of the white robe of the Old Testament high priest (cf. i); and within the Roman Catholic Church in Madagascar one can find examples of traditional Malagasy burial rites being used with reference to the Genesis narrative about how Jacob was transferred to Canaan after his death (cf. ii).

13 For a discussion of the problems created by a theological training in the West—which then is to be put into practice in Africa, cf. J.S. Ukpong, "Rereading the Bible with African eyes", *Journal of Theology for Southern Africa* 91 (1995) 3–14.

14 The general bibliography on African theology by J.U. Young III, *African theology. A critical analysis and annotated bibliography* (1993), has few references to biblical interpretation; for more specialised bibliographies, cf. G. LeMarquand, "A bibliography of the Bible in Africa", *Bulletin for Contextual Theology* 2/II (1995) 6–40; and K. Holter, *Tropical Africa and the Old Testament* (1996). The new University of Stellenbosch database on the Bible in Africa will here represent a

scattered attempts at analysing research historical lines;[15] still, a lot remains to be done. Let me, just to exemplify this, single out one particular question that, as far as I'm concerned, clearly needs further attention, namely why African biblical scholars have focused so strongly on comparative studies that relate the biblical texts and the African experience. I have recently suggested that this is not only a result of the contextual approach of popular interpretation; rather, I have argued, it also reflects two other circumstances. One is the deficient infrastructure of African research institutions. What else can an African biblical scholar make use of, in his or her interpretation, than the only material that is available in the seminary or university library, that is the African comparative material?[16] But I have also suggested—and it is here I think there is a need for further and more fundamental research—that this interest for reading the Bible in the light of African comparative material reflects the intellectual and institutional context of early post-colonial

---

breakthrough; for a presentation, cf. W.R. Kawale, "New data base: Bible in Africa research project", *Newsletter on African Old Testament Scholarship* 3 (1997) 3–4.

15 For early surveys, cf. J.S. Mbiti, "The biblical basis in present trends of African theology", *Africa Theological Journal* 7/1 (1978) 72–85; N. Onwu, "The current state of biblical studies in Africa", *Journal of Religious Thought* 41 (1985) 35–46; and S.O. Abogunrin, "Biblical research in Africa: The task ahead", *Africa Journal of Biblical Studies* 1/1 (1986) 7–24. More recent contributions are R.G. Rogers, "Biblical hermeneutics and contemporary African theology", L.M. Hopfe (ed.), *Uncovering ancient stones* (1994) 245–260; G.O. West, "On the eve of an African biblical studies: Trajectories and trends", *Journal of Theology for Southern Africa* 99 (1997) 99–115; and K. Holter, "It's not only a question of money! African Old Testament scholarship between the myths and meanings of the South and the money and methods of the North", *Old Testament Essays* 11 (1998) 240–254; *idem*, "Old Testament scholarship in Sub-Saharan Africa", G.O. West & M.W. Dube (eds.), *The Bible in Africa* (2000); and J. Punt, "Reading the Bible in Africa: Accounting for some trends (Part I)", *Scriptura* 68 (1999) 1–11.

16 The deficient infrastructure is discussed in D.T. Adamo, "Doing Old Testament research in Africa", *Newsletter on African Old Testament Scholarship* 3 (1997) 8–11; and K. Holter, "It's not only a question of money! African Old Testament scholarship between the myths and meanings of the South and the money and methods of the North", *Old Testament Essays* 11 (1998) 240–254. With regard to the library situation, cf. also J. Muutuki, "Library resources for Old Testament research in Nairobi", *Newsletter on African Old Testament Scholarship* 3 (1997) 5–7; and D.N. Bowen, "Old Testament literature in the NEGST library", *Newsletter on African Old Testament Scholarship* 4 (1998) 20–21.

Africa, and its deliberate policy of developing africanised scholarly approaches.[17]

Interaction between the two contexts—and their interpretations

Let me go on to say some words about the interaction between these two contexts of biblical interpretation in Africa, the popular one and the academic one, and their respective interpretations. It should here be remembered that most of us actually belong to both contexts. On the one hand, we have come together here in Stellenbosch because we are professional interpreters of the Bible. We have an academic training in biblical interpretation, and we have even made a living out of interpreting the Bible professionally. On the other hand, however, we are also familiar with different kinds of popular interpretations of the Bible. Our first experiences with the Bible were certainly in a popular context, and we train people for different kinds of services in the same. At least in our case it is a question of different functions, rather than different persons. In other words, the traditional dichotomy between the two sets of contexts and interpretations needs to be questioned.[18]

Parallel structures
It should here be noted that these two sets of contexts and interpretations have quite parallel structures, as both experience a tension between universal and contextual aspects. The universal aspects of the popular context and its interpretation reflects the universal aspect of the biblical texts themselves and (or perhaps in the opposite order!) of Christianity in its historical and denominational expressions, whereas the universal aspect of the academic context and its interpretation in addition reflects the strong influence of the western guild of biblical scholarship. With regard to the contextual aspects, both wish to give an interpretation that relates the biblical texts to the African context. The popular context and its interpretation does so intuitively, and without addressing the problem

---

[17] Cf. K. Holter, "The institutional context of Old Testament scholarship in Africa", *Old Testament Essays* 11 (1998) 452–461; cf. also F.E. Deist, "Biblical interpretation in post-colonial Africa", *Svensk Teologisk Kvartalskrift* 72 (1996) 110–118.

[18] Cf. T.M. Hinga, "'Reading with': An exploration of the interface between 'critical' and 'ordinary' readings of the Bible: A response", *Semeia* 73 (1996) 283–284.

directly, whereas the academic context and its interpretation certainly addresses the problem; partly at a theoretical level, as a number of scholars have emphasised contextualised interpretations as a research political priority of African biblical scholarship,[19] and partly at a practical level, as contextualised interpretations actually have received most of the attention from African biblical scholars.[20]

Models for interaction

These parallels reflect the ongoing interaction between the two contexts and their respective interpretations. Let me, in an attempt at describing this interaction, draw two different models.

First, there is what I will call a *dominance* model. This is a model where the two contexts and their interpretations struggle to establish dominance over each other. It could be the popular context and interpretation trying to dominate the academic one. The examples here are many. Lay interpreters are frightened by the fragmentation of the word of God that seems to be advocated by the professionals, and in an attempt to save the Bible they try to suppress the interpretation of these professionals.[21] Or, it could be the academic context and interpretation trying to dominate the popular one. Also here the examples are many. The professionals see the naive interpretations of certain biblical texts by the laity, and in an attempt to save the lay interpreters, the church, or even the biblical texts themselves, from the dangers of fundamentalism, they offer scholarly help from the critical interpretations of the same texts.[22]

---

19 This is expressed in some research historical articles, such as N. Onwu, "The current state of biblical studies in Africa", *Journal of Religious Thought* 41 (1985) 35–46; and S.O. Abogunrin, "Biblical research in Africa: The task ahead", *Africa Journal of Biblical Studies* 1/I (1986) 7–24. However, the same is also expressed in the policy statement of *African Journal of Biblical Studies* (printed in every issue of the journal), which says that one aims to: "Encourage biblical scholars to look afresh at the Bible with an African insight, and relate their interpretation to the past and the prevailing situation in Africa. "

20 Cf. K. Holter, *Tropical Africa and the Old Testament* (1996) *passim*.

21 Classical areas of tension known from the West are also reflected in Africa; for example the historicity of the Jonah and Elisha narratives.

22 Cf. for example C.U. Manus, "Elijah—a *nabi* before the 'writing prophets': Some critical reflections", *African Journal of Biblical Studies* 1/I (1986) 31, who argues that an historical-critical study of the Elijah-narrative provides a paradigm for African 'prophets'; rather than engaging in popular 'fortune-telling' and 'power

Secondly, and indeed more relevant, is what I will call a *complementary* model. This is a model where the two contexts and their interpretations acknowledge each other as equal participants—although with different contributions to make—in the joint enterprise of creating an understanding of what the word of God means for people of today. One way is to bridge the gap between the two from both sides at the same time; a forum for exposing the existential and religious emphasis of the popular context and the critical emphasis of the academic context to each other is then to be created.[23] Another way is to let the experience of the professional context participate and facilitate the interpretation process of the popular context.[24] In both cases South African biblical scholars play an important role, and it is to hoped that some of their models (and caution!) can be tried out and reflected upon also north of the Zambezi.

Conclusion

Let me return to the East African village woman; the one that walks around always carrying her Bible, pointing out that the Bible is not only a book we can read, it is also a book that reads us. Without the slightest

---

tussle' they are challenged to be 'the conscience of the people'. Even harsher is K. Owan, "The fundamentalist's interpretation of the Bible: A challenge to biblical exegetes in West Africa", *West African Journal of Ecclesial Studies* 5 (1993) 1, who argues that critical scholarship is necessary to fight fundamentalism, "one of the plagues now overwhelming the Church".

23 Cf. L.C. Jonker, "Bridging the gap between Bible readers and 'professional' exegetes", *Old Testament Essays* 10 (1997) 69–83; cf. also E.M. Conradie, "Tracy's notion of dialogue: 'Our last, best hope'?", *Scriptura* 57 (1996) 149–178; and F.E. Deist, *Ervaring, rede en metode in Skrifuitleg* (1994) 329–342.

24 A leading proponent here i G.O. West; cf. his "Difference and dialogue: Reading the Joseph story with poor and marginalised communities in South Africa", *Biblical Interpretation* 2 (1994) 152–170; "Reading the Bible differently: Giving shape to the discourse of the dominated", *Semeia* 73 (1996) 21–41; and most recently, *The Academy of the Poor: Towards a Dialogical Reading of the Bible* (1999). West's approach has received much attention, cf. J.A. Draper, "Confessional Western text-centered biblical interpretation and oral or residual-oral context", *Semeia* 73 (1996) 59–77; B.C. Lategan, "Scholar and ordinary reader—more than a simple interface", *Semeia* 73 (1996) 243–255; and G.F. Snyman, "'Ilahle Elinothuthu'? The lay reader and/or the critical reader—some remarks on africanisation", *Religion & Theology* 6 (1999) 140–167.

knowledge about names and positions in the contemporary hermeneutical discussion, she intuitively experiences some of the interaction between context and interpretation.

Our obligation as biblical scholars—I would argue—is to create a context for biblical interpretation, where her popular and our academic experiences can meet and interact in mutual respect. We have the influence that is needed to initiate the research and establish the teaching programs that will let the interpretations of the popular and academic contexts fruitfully interact.[25] So, let us return to our universities and seminaries and do it!

---

[25] A preliminary discussion of the implications of this with regard to teaching programs is found in S. Gitau, & al., "Contextualized Old Testament programmes?", *Newsletter on African Old Testament Scholarship* 2 (1997) 3–7.

• 5 •

Ancient Israel and Modern Nigeria
Some Remarks from the Sidelines on the Socio-critical Aspect of Nigerian Old Testament Scholarship

Coming from a tradition of Old Testament scholarship which generally would hesitate to participate in the current socio-ethical and socio-political debate, I have found it both interesting and challenging to meet the African branch of Old Testament scholarship, where the opposite often is the case; scholars frankly enter the current socio-ethical and socio-political debate with the firm conviction that they—as Old Testament scholars—have something to contribute to this debate.[1] As Nigerian scholars play a major role in African Old Testament scholarship in general, it is hardly surprising to find that this tendency of socio-critical awareness is reflected in their scholarly production. And when the annual conference of the Nigerian Association for Biblical Studies this year has chosen "Biblical Principles as Moral Foundation for the Nigerian Society" as its major theme, I will use the opportunity to make a few remarks—and as a foreigner these remarks will indeed be from the sidelines—on this socio-critical aspect of Nigerian Old Testament

---

1   Paper read at the Annual Conference of the Nigerian Association for Biblical Studies, Owerri (Nigeria), October 1995.

Scholarship. I will do so by presenting and commenting upon two articles, written by two different Nigerian scholars. Both articles were published in 1986 in the first volume of the *African Journal of Biblical Studies*, issued by your own Nigerian Association for Biblical Studies.[2]

The two articles to be discussed include one by Gabriel O. Abe on the theological significance of *bᵉrît* / covenant in ancient Israel and in modern Nigeria, and one by Chris U. Manus on the prophet Elijah as a model for prophets and social critics in contemporary Africa.[3] Although these two articles deal with quite different issues, they reveal a common interest for relating Old Testament issues to corresponding issues in contemporary Nigerian and African society, and as such they can be dealt with together. It should be emphasised that these two contributions by no means stand alone; one could easily point out a number of other contributions reflecting similar approaches, by the same two scholars,[4] as well as by others,[5] or one could just consult the theme of this conference. However, for obvious reasons it is impossible to make any exhaustive analysis in a paper like this, and the ones to be analysed in the following should, hopefully, suffice to exemplify what I shall hereafter refer to as the socio-critical aspect of Nigerian Old Testament scholarship.

The paper is divided into two parts. The first gives a presentation of the two articles. Then follows a closer analysis, where I attempt to expose the purpose and methods used in the two articles, and where I will also relate the articles to a wider hermeneutical setting, confronting them with the bi-polar hermeneutical paradigm of African theology described by the African American theologian Josiah U. Young.

---

[2]   Nearly a decade has now passed since this first volume of *African Journal of Biblical Studies* was launched (1986), and let the following remarks be my way of paying tribute to a journal which is of utmost importance for the development of an independent Biblical scholarship in Africa.

[3]   G.O. Abe, "Berith: Its impact on Israel and its relevance to the Nigerian society", *African Journal of Biblical Studies* 1/I (1986) 66–73; C.U. Manus, "Elijah—a *nabi'* before the 'writing prophets'", *African Journal of Biblical Studies* 1/I (1986) 25–34.

[4]   Cf. for example G.O. Abe, "Religion and national unity", *Africa Theological Journal* 15 (1986) 63–72.

[5]   Cf. for example A.O. Onah, "Prophet Ezekiel's concept of individuality: Guidelines for Nigeria", *African Journal of Biblical Studies* 6/II (1991) 68–78; D.A. Olubunmo, "Israelite concept of ideal king", *African Journal of Biblical Studies* 6/II (1991) 59–67.

Presentation of the two articles

G.O. Abe: The covenant in ancient Israel—and in Nigeria
In the first article, G.O. Abe studies the Old Testament concept of b^e*rît* /
covenant. Abe initially says that he wants to:

> [...] discuss the term in its religious sense and especially its impact on
> the social set up of ancient Israel and the relevance to the Nigerian
> Society.[6]

After a general presentation of the Old Testament concept of the b^e*rît*
between Yahweh and Israel, Abe notices four areas where the b^e*rît* was
violated in ancient Israel, and in each area he draws lines to today's
Nigeria. The first area concerns politics. Arguing that Israel both
politically and technologically was a developing nation, Abe notices how
David and Solomon got technological aid from neighbouring kings, and
how this enabled them to achieve both national growth and international
recognition. This, however, led to a neglect of Yahweh and to the
adoption of foreign gods, and the violation of the b^e*rît* ultimately led to
the catastrophes in 721 and 587. Abe then claims this political aspect of
the b^e*rît* to have relevance for contemporary Nigeria:

> During the last electioneering campaigns in Nigeria, the various
> political parties had laudable manifestos which was [sic] presented on
> the rostrum with sugary tongues. [...] During this period, the
> politicians entered into what one might term some form of covenant
> with the people of Nigeria. [...] But as soon as they got into power,
> they indifferently violated most of the agreed terms, under which they
> were elected to rule.[7]

The second area of violation of the b^e*rît* concerns economy. Abe
refers to the Old Testament picture of the people of Israel as living an
agricultural mode of life, where the land which they cultivated belonged
to Yahweh, and the crops which they planted were made productive by
his divine providence. When Israel failed to recognise or worship
Yahweh, the land would suffer economically. One example of this is the
economic prosperity of the eighth century, which was accompanied by

---

[6]   Cf. G.O. Abe, "Berith", *African Journal of Biblical Studies* 1/I (1986) 66.

[7]   Cf. *ibid.*, 69–70.

social injustices and moral decadence. According to the Old Testament this prepared for the Assyrian conquest of Israel in 722 BC, a catastrophe interpreted as the judgement of Yahweh. Another example is the post-exilic negligence of re-building the temple, which, it is argued, made Yahweh withhold the dew in heaven and the products of the earth. Also this economical aspect of the $b^e r\hat{\imath}t$ is claimed to have relevance for Nigeria, and Abe argues that in spite of being an agriculturally fertile land, Nigeria may plunge herself into total economic chaos, due to fraud, extravagant spending, and embezzlement of public funds.[8]

The third and fourth areas of violation of the $b^e r\hat{\imath}t$ concerns domestic and educational matters, and also here Abe draws lines between ancient Israel and today's Nigeria. In the former he points out that the violation of marital laws in ancient Israel has parallels in the many broken marriages in Nigeria, and in the latter he emphasises the importance of education in both societies.[9]

C.U. Manus: Elijah—as a paradigm for African prophets

The second contribution reflects a similar socio-critical approach to the Old Testament. C.U. Manus focuses upon the prophet Elijah, and his major point is that this prophet could serve as a model for African "prophets" of today.[10]

Initially Manus provides some background information about the historical setting of the prophet and the literary setting of the so-called Elijah cycles, but the major focus of the article is on one particular element of these cycles, the narrative about Elijah at Horeb in 1 Kings 19:1–18. Manus divides this passage into three parts; vv. 1–7, where Elijah is depicted as a fugitive from Jezebel's wrath, vv. 8–14, where the prophet arrives at Mount Horeb and meets God, and vv. 15–18, where Elijah is commissioned to anoint Hazael as king of Aram, Jehu as king of Israel, and Elisha to succeed himself as prophet. This tripartite structure of the passage is then claimed to provide a key to its meaning, as each unit gives the impression of a different tradition, worked together and stylistically coloured by the Deuteronomistic redactors.[11] The two first units, vv. 1–7 and 8–14, depict a situation of crisis. The location at

---

8   Cf. *ibid.*, 70–71.

9   Cf. *ibid.*, 71–72.

10   Cf. C.U. Manus, "Elijah", *African Journal of Biblical Studies* 1/1 (1986) 25–34.

11   Cf. *ibid.*, 29.

Mount Horeb, and also the theophany, probably refer to Moses, and the reader gets the impression that what had begun with Moses is now falling apart. Divine intervention is therefore needed, and the function of the final unit, vv. 15–18, is to describe this intervention. The prophet is called to participate in the political struggle of his time, by anointing Hazael, Jehu, and Elisha. Formed as an oracle of doom, vv. 15–18 then describe how the prophet is called to execute the sentence given by Yahweh.

The latter aspect of the narrative about Elijah at Mount Horeb, namely the intervention of the prophet in the political struggle of his time, is especially emphasised by Manus, who uses this aspect as a basis for a contextualisation of the narrative. Accusing contemporary African prophets of confounding their audience with unpalatable "visions", at the cost of Elijah's "political" aspect, Manus asks how the audience may authenticate the claims of "visions", as these are never corroborated with historical happenings. In this respect the prophet Elijah

> [...] provides a paradigm for our local 'prophets' who seem to engage rather in 'fortune-telling' and 'power tussle' in their various Churches and communities than being 'the conscience of the people'.[12]

This aspect of prophecy, being "the conscience of the people" rather than providing the people with sensational "visions", is then identified by Manus as the call to speak out, fierce and fearless, against any situation where justice and right are trampled and where the poor and the underprivileged are being oppressed. Or, in other words:

> It is one thing to claim to be a God-sent and God-inspired prophet and act in the OT prophetic fashion to bamboozle the schizophrenically religious and it is another to live out fully the characteristic traits of a living prophet of God.[13]

---

[12] *Ibid.*, 31.

[13] *Ibid.*, 32. For another contribution with a similar emphasis, cf. M. Ita, "Biblical prophecy and its challenge to contemporary prophetic movements", *Africa Theological Journal* 18 (1989) 3–16.

Analysis of the two articles

After this brief presentation of the two articles, I would like to make some critical remarks on their motivation, their methodology, and their wider hermeneutical setting.

Motivation
Why, then, this interest in relating Old Testament texts and motifs to issues in the contemporary Nigerian context? The question probably reveals my non-African background. As I said in the opening of this paper, I come from a tradition of Old Testament scholarship which generally would hesitate to participate in the current socio-ethical and socio-political debate; while, as it seems to me, African colleagues often have an opposite approach, frankly entering this debate.

Their socio-critical approach has a double function. On the one hand, they explicitly condemn any oppression of the people. Abe speaks very directly, claiming that:

> In fact, since the Nigerian Independence in 1960, the country has ever been subjected to political slavery of both the civilian and the military governments.[14]

But Manus is equally clear, when he argues that:

> African 'prophets' and social critics as well, in order to promote orderly social transformations, must speak out today and at all times against our multifarious social ills; against all forms of oppression and man's inhumanity to man.[15]

On the other hand, however, they both express an almost patriotic approach, as it seems to be a major concern of theirs to encourage individual Christians and the church to play a constructive role in the work for a better society. Abe emphasises the value of a god-fearing population:

---

14   G.O. Abe, "Berith", *African Journal of Biblical Studies* 1/I (1986) 70.

15   C.U. Manus, "Elijah", *African Journal of Biblical Studies* 1/I (1986) 32.

This will make the various manufacturers and employers of labour contribute faithfully to the national development.[16]

Something of the same is reflected in Manus's article:

> The patriotic concern of prophet Elijah, his struggle against religious apartheid in Israel, all point to the weight the redactors put on the deep religious experience of the prophet. This single trait in prophet Elijah provides a paradigm for our local 'prophets'.[17]

Accordingly, although one could get a rather negative impression when Abe points out a series of parallels of how both ancient Israel and modern Nigeria violate the $b^e r \hat{i} t$, I believe his concern is the very opposite; the paralleling of the two reflects an optimistic challenge to his contemporaries to obedience, rather than to a pessimistic acceptance of the violation, and as such Abe has a positive message to his fellow Nigerians. Similarly, when Manus complains that society becomes amoral when prophets go silent, it represents an optimistic challenge to African prophets and social critics. As they speak out against all forms of oppression, they actually contribute to the building of a better society.

Methodological approach

How, then, do Abe and Manus approach their task? What is their methodology? One could obviously say that the question of methodology by no means is an urgent one, since application of Old Testament texts and motifs in the life of both individuals and society is hardly a new enterprise. It is of course true that the church has always read the ancient texts into new contexts, and, likewise, that systematic theologians have always related Scripture to contemporary ethical, philosophical, and sociological issues. However, it should be emphasised that both Abe and Manus approach this topic as biblical scholars, and not, or at least not primarily, as ordained ministers or systematic theologians. This is quite obvious in Abe's case, as his article is built on his Ibadan Ph.D. thesis on the covenant in the Old Testament,[18] but also Manus's article reflects the skill of a biblical scholar well acquainted with the recent discussion of

---

[16] G.O. Abe, "Berith", *African Journal of Biblical Studies* 1/I (1986) 69.

[17] C.U. Manus, "Elijah", *African Journal of Biblical Studies* 1/I (1986) 31.

[18] G.O. Abe, *Covenant in the Old Testament* (1983); for an abstract, cf. *African Journal of Biblical Studies* 1 /II (1986) 183.

his topic within biblical scholarship. Thus, Abe and Manus approach the current socio-critical debate, with their training as biblical scholars as luggage. Abe argues that he wants to:

> [...] discuss the term [i.e. $b^e r\hat{\imath}t$] in its religious sense and especially its impact on the social set up of ancient Israel and its relevance to the Nigerian Society.[19]

And the same is expressed by Manus, as he explains his motivation for writing the article:

> (a) Bearing in mind how the general public in every African nation is daily fed with 'sensational prophecies' and how many of these so-called 'revelations' and 'visions' have proved unfulfilled and unrealistic, the public mind needs to be disabused. (b) And aware of an increasing return to the importance of prophecy in contemporary Biblical Theology, an African side of the story has long been a *desideratum*.[20]

Accordingly, the two articles reflect the deliberate intention of Abe and Manus to take biblical scholarship into the service of the current socio-critical debate. Hence my question about their methodology: How do they approach this topic?

Nigerian scholars of religion are well known for their comparative approach to the three major religious traditions in Nigeria, African traditional religion, Christianity, and Islam. As for example is expressed in the "Statement of purpose" in *Orita*, one aims at studying these three religious traditions "[...] insofar as there has been cross-fertilization between them", and further, one wants to "[...] encourage articles which treat their interaction."[21] This comparative approach is also reflected in Nigerian Old Testament scholarship. I do not know how many articles comparing Old Testament issues with corresponding issues for example in the Yoruba or Igbo traditions have been published, but they seem to be

---

19 G.O. Abe, "Berith", *African Journal of Biblical Studies* 1/I (1986) 66.

20 C.U. Manus, "Elijah", *African Journal of Biblical Studies* 1/I (1986) 25.

21 Cf. "Statement of Purpose", printed at the colophon page in every issue of *Orita: Ibadan Journal of Religious Studies*, published by the Department of Religious Studies, University of Ibadan.

numerous.[22] Abe and Manus have also participated in this enterprise; as examples I could mention an article by Abe from 1989, where he studies the relationship between the social institution of marriage in the Old Testament and among the Yoruba, and an article by Manus from 1986, where he studies the relationship between the concepts of death and the afterlife in the Old Testament and in Igbo traditional religion.[23]

Now, the question here is whether the socio-critical articles by Abe and Manus reflect the same methodological approach as their religio-cultural articles do. The question is interesting, both because scholars favouring religio-cultural questions traditionally have been quite reluctant to deal with socio-critical questions,[24] but also because scholars favouring socio-critical questions have been equally reluctant to deal with what F.E. Boulaga, somewhat ironically, has called "[...] local curiosities, folklore, or peculiarities of a lifestyle that have disappeared or are barely surviving".[25] Let me therefore make three remarks on the relationship between the two socio-critical articles discussed in this paper, and the two other articles by the same authors, just mentioned.

Firstly, the methodological problem of any sort of comparison: the need to know both fields equally well. It has been emphasised by advocates of religio-cultural comparisons that those who engage in comparisons between the Old Testament and traditional African religion and culture, need to have studied both seriously.[26] Now, this is obviously very demanding, and few scholars are actually specialists in more than one academic field. But what clearly is needed is some methodological awareness. In this respect Abe and Manus seem to express a similar attitude in both sets of articles. Although they primarily are biblical scholars, one finds references to scholarly studies in the Yoruba and Igbo

---

22 Let me here (in addition to those referred to in note 23) mention just two contributions to exemplify this: E.D. Adelowo, "A comparative study of creation stories in Yoruba religion, Islam and Judaeo-Christianity", *Africa Theological Journal* 15 (1986) 29–53; G.E. Okeke, "Concepts of future life: Biblical and Igbo", *Neue Zeitschrift für Missionswissenschaft* 44 (1988) 178–196.

23 Cf. G.O. Abe, "The Jewish and Yoruba social institution of marriage", *Orita* 21 (1989) 3–18; C.U. Manus, "The concept of death and the after-life in the Old Testament and Igbo traditional religion", *Mission Studies* 3/2 (1986) 41–56.

24 See K.A. Dickson, *Theology in Africa* (1984) 108–140.

25 F.E. Boulaga, *Christianity without fetishes* (1984) 57.

26 Cf. for example S.O. Abogunrin, "Biblical research in Africa", *African Journal of Biblical Studies* 1/I (1986) 15.

religious traditions in their religio-cultural articles, as well as references
to sociological studies in their socio-critical articles.[27]

Secondly, the question of motivation needs to be mentioned here
too, since both sets of articles seem to reflect a parallel way of
expressing the motivation. In his socio-critical article Abe says that he
wants to point out what can be of "[...] relevance to the Nigerian
Society",[28] and in his religio-cultural article he aims at formulating "[...]
an ideal African theology of marriage [...]".[29] Manus expresses his
motivation in an even closer language. In his socio-critical article he
argues that he wants to show how Elijah's theology can be
contextualised in contemporary Africa,[30] and in his religio-cultural
article he argues that such studies are necessary to meet the demands for
inculturation (for example) in Africa.[31]

Finally, the actual comparison. Although Abe, in his socio-critical
article on $b^e r\hat{\imath}t$, again and again makes comparisons between ancient
Israel and modern Nigeria, he actually never explicitly describes this
enterprise. Nevertheless, the repeated thought-form throughout the article
is "Nigeria, like ancient Israel".[32] However, in his religio-cultural article
on the social institution of marriage in the Old Testament and among the
Yoruba, he has a similar series of comparisons, and here he also
explicitly says that he wants to make a comparison:

---

27   Cf. G.O. Abe, "The Jewish and Yoruba social institution of marriage", *Orita* 21
     (1989) notes 14 ff.; *idem*, "Berith", *African Journal of Biblical Studies* 1/I (1986)
     notes 12–13; C.U. Manus, "The concept of death and the after-life in the Old
     Testament and Igbo traditional religion", *Mission Studies* 3/2 (1986) notes 51 ff.;
     idem, "Elijah", *African Journal of Biblical Studies* 1/I (1986) note 1.

28   G.O. Abe, "Berith", *African Journal of Biblical Studies* 1/I (1986) 66.

29   G.O. Abe, "The Jewish and Yoruba social institution of marriage", *Orita* 21 (1989)
     18.

30   C.U. Manus, "Elijah", *African Journal of Biblical Studies* 1/I (1986) 26.

31   C.U. Manus, "The concept of death and the after-life in the Old Testament and Igbo
     traditional religion", *Mission Studies* 3/2 (1986) 53.

32   Cf. for example G.O. Abe, "Berith", *African Journal of Biblical Studies* 1/I (1986)
     69.

This article examines the Jewish concepts of marriage from the ancient times as related to Yoruba features. Making a comparative appraisal of this social institution in the cultures of both societies.[33]

Turning over to Manus, we notice that throughout his socio-critical article he compares the prophet Elijah again and again with contemporary African prophets; as for example when the narrative about Elijah in the desert is used to say that:

This wilderness experience [...] is indeed a *sine qua non* for the development and nurture of authentic African prophetism in our times.[34]

The same comparative approach is reflected also in his religio-cultural article on the concept of death and after-life in the Old Testament and in Igbo traditional religion; he explicitly says that he wants to compare the two religious traditions:

I will present some reflections on the outstanding comparative features from both religious thought-forms [...].[35]

Thus, after this survey it should be clear that there are no major methodological differences between the socio-critical studies by Abe and Manus, discussed in the present paper, and other publications of theirs, where they, according to the more traditional comparative approach, make comparisons between religio-cultural features in ancient Israel and in traditional Africa.

Wider hermeneutical setting
Finally, some words should also be said about the wider hermeneutical setting of the two articles in question; and the topic to be discussed, briefly, is the following: How do they relate to more general streams in African hermeneutics?

---

[33] G.O. Abe, "The Jewish and Yoruba social institution of marriage", *Orita* 21 (1989) 3.

[34] C.U. Manus, "Elijah", *African Journal of Biblical Studies* 1/I (1986) 31.

[35] C.U. Manus, "The concept of death and the after-life in the Old Testament and Igbo traditional religion", *Mission Studies* 3/2 (1986) 41.

In the vast area of African hermeneutics, an important means of orientation has recently been provided by the African American theologian Josiah U. Young, who in his monograph *African theology: A critical analysis and annotated bibliography* (1993), introduces a bi-polar hermeneutical paradigm.[36] On the one hand Young identifies what he calls the "old guard", that is scholars such as B. Idowu, J. Mbiti, and H. Sawyer, arguing that these focused primarily on religio-cultural analysis, seeking to expose continuities and discontinuities between African traditional religion and Christian faith.[37] This focusing on religio-cultural analysis, he claims, was made at the cost of a socio-critical analysis sensitive to present political problems. Writing in the 1960s and 1970s these scholars assumed most of Africa to have gained independence; or, as Young somewhat ironically puts it, they believed in the "myth of independence" promulgated by the westernised and educated African elite.[38] Hence, a socio-critical analysis was no longer considered necessary.[39] On the other hand Young identifies what he calls the "new guard", that is scholars such as J.-M. Éla, E. Mveng, E. Boulaga, B. Adoukonou, and M.A. Oduyoye, arguing that these are far more committed to socio-critical analysis; these, however, do so at the cost of the religio-cultural analysis. Writing in the 1980s, more or less in response to the South African call for liberation, these scholars, he claims, realise the apartheid of South Africa to be just one aspect of the more general neo-colonialism still plaguing most of Africa, and hence the call for liberation is extended throughout the whole of Africa.

Accordingly, Young presents a chronologically based paradigm. He claims that the 1980s marks a turning point in African hermeneutics,

---

36   J.U. Young III, *African theology* (1993) 13–33; cf. also his "African theology: From independence to liberation", *Voices from the third world* 10/4 (1987) 41–48, where the same distinction is presented more briefly.

37   J.U. Young III, *African theology* (1993) 23.

38   *Ibid.*, 13.

39   Although not referred to by Young, I believe this notion is expressed most explicitly by K.A. Dickson, *Theology in Africa* (1984) 133: "Another reason why the present tendency among theologians from outside South Africa to have a preponderantly cultural approach to theologising is that most of Black Africa is ruled by Black Africans; the colonial situation exists in only a few African countries, notably South Africa, the great majority of African countries having achieved independence from their erstwhile colonial rulers, so that for the latter there is no question of Whites oppressing Blacks. "

since the inculturation hermeneutics of the "old guard", which focused on religio-cultural analysis, is replaced by the liberation hermeneutics of the "new guard", focusing on socio-critical analysis. Let us then compare this paradigm of Young to the two articles by Abe and Manus. It should be admitted that neither of them are actually listed in Young's bibliography; in fact, he seems to be surprisingly unaware of the *African Journal of Biblical Studies*. Nevertheless, it should be relevant to make such a comparison, since the articles in question both chronologically and thematically belong to Young's "new guard"; chronologically as they originate in the 1980s, and thematically as they reflect a socio-critical focusing. One should then expect that they would also reflect the hermeneutical basis of the "new guard". Let me, however, point out two features which demonstrates that this hardly is the case.

First, we have already noticed that the articles by Abe and Manus methodologically reflect the traditional comparative approach. As pointed out above, I have not been able to find any methodological differences between their socio-critical studies and other publications of theirs, where they, according to the more traditional comparative approach, make comparisons between religio-cultural features in ancient Israel and in traditional Africa.

Secondly, one should notice that the articles by Abe and Manus, although they focus upon socio-critical questions, actually reveal no signs of the liberation motif, which is the hermeneutical basis of the socio-critical focusing of Young's "new guard". This can be seen in two ways. First, the contributions by Abe and Manus lack the liberation motif as such. This is quite surprising, since both emphasise the oppression motif, which is a basic premise for the liberation motif. But in the case of Abe and Manus the oppression motif never leads to the liberation motif. Secondly, neither of them have any references to literature by theologians promoting liberation hermeneutics. This is equally surprising. The South African focus on liberation hermeneutics, initially represented by names such as for example D. Tutu and A. Boesak,[40] was soon to be echoed outside South Africa, also in the writings of important

---

40 For surveys, cf. J. Mosala, *Biblical hermeneutics and black theology in South Africa* (1989); G.O. West, *Biblical hermeneutics of liberation* (1995).

West African theologians such as for example J.-M. Ela[41] or M.A. Oduyoye;[42] not, however, in the two contributions by Abe and Manus.

Accordingly, the publications by G. Abe and C.U. Manus from the latter part of the 1980s demonstrate clearly that what I have called the socio-critical aspect of Nigerian Old Testament scholarship seems to be going its own way, regardless of any supposed division between a religio-cultural analysis of an "old guard" vs a socio-critical analysis of a "new guards". Abe's and Manus' methodology echo the former, their questions echo the latter, and their answers are their own. Let me make two comments on this.

First, as far as Young's paradigm is concerned, it remains a basic problem that his distinction between an "old guard" and a "new guard" inevitably implies the idea of a chronological development. The distinction between the 1960s and 1970s vs the 1980s obviously have chronological connotations, and the very terms "old" vs "new", where Young clearly favours the latter, connects this chronological concept with the concept of a development. However, as pointed out quite recently by R.G. Rogers, in a critical review of Young's paradigm, there is no such exclusively chronological line of demarcation between African theologians writing in the 1960s and 1970s, and the ones writing in the 1980s. Those theologians selected by Young to represent the 1980s are influenced by certain perceptions of political and social conditions in Africa. One could, however, easily point out examples of other theologians, also active in the 1980s, who were influenced by other considerations.[43] The two articles by Abe and Manus, I would argue, could serve as such examples. Although they both chronologically and thematically belong to Young's "new guard", their approach reflect the inculturation hermeneutics which traditionally has dominated Nigerian Old Testament scholarship, rather than the liberation hermeneutics. Thus, Young's paradigm is not fully relevant; African hermeneutics, as demonstrated by two examples of Nigerian Old Testament scholarship, is

---

41   J.-M. Ela, *Le cri de l'homme africain* (1980); cf. for example pp. 40–51, where he makes "an African reading of Exodus".

42   M.A. Oduyoye, *Hearing and knowing* (1986); cf. for example pp. 79–89, where she uses the exodus event of the Old Testament as a paradigm for contemporary African theology.

43   R.G. Rogers, "Biblical hermeneutics and contemporary African theology", L.M. Hopfe (ed.), *Uncovering ancient stones* (1994) 259.

a far too complex entity to fit into a dividing between an "old guard" and a "new guard".

Secondly, the hermeneutical approach of Abe and Manus from the mid-80s, where they have a common approach to socio-critical and religio-cultural questions, seems to be an anticipation of an hermeneutical approach coming now in the mid-90s. J.S. Pobee has earlier this year argued that:

> Earlier on it used to be said that the two hermeneutics were distinct. Today the two are being seen as complementary.[44]

And a similar expression grew out of the Glasgow consultation on "Interpreting the Bible in African contexts" last year:

> Perhaps the most creative moment of the consultation was the realisation that cultural reading need to reflect the socio-economic context of particular communities; just as those who have been pursuing a hermeneutic in Southern Africa driven principally by socio-economic concerns, are now, since the elections, turning to questions of Africanisation.[45]

A final remark

In the opening of this paper I said that I come from a tradition of Old Testament scholarship which generally would hesitate to participate in the current socio-ethical and socio-political debate, and that I have therefore found it both interesting and challenging to meet the African branch of Old Testament scholarship, where the opposite often is the case. In July this year (1995) two major congresses for Biblical scholars took place in Europe; first the International Organisation for the Study of the Old Testament met in Cambridge, UK, and then the Society of Biblical Literature met in Budapest, Hungary. Attending the first of these

---

[44]   J.S. Pobee, "The use of the Bible in African theology", T. Fornberg (ed.), *Bible, hermeneutics, mission* (1995) 121.

[45]   J. Riches, "Interpreting the Bible in African contexts", *Ministerial Formation* 67 (1994) 58–59. For a South African contribution pointing in the same direction, cf. F. Deist, "South African Old Testament studies and the future", *Old Testament Essays* 5 (1992) 311–331.

two congresses I got a somewhat untraditional idea: What if the organisers had borrowed the theme of the annual conference of the Nigerian Association for Biblical Studies? It could have been formulated in the following way: "Biblical principles as moral foundations—in a new Europe". That would certainly have been an important topic, and I am also sure that European Old Testament scholars would have had much to contribute to this topic.

By this I do not suggest that Old Testament scholars should abandon exegetical and theological questions, and concentrate on the current socio-critical debate alone. A socio-critical approach is hardly any "shibboleth" to the Old Testament texts, and vice versa, the Old Testament texts can hardly be any "shibboleth" in the current socio-critical debate. Nevertheless, an ideal could perhaps be "to practice the latter, without neglecting the former" (Math 23:23). And as far as this is concerned, I believe Old Testament scholars would benefit from listening, not only to the voices from Cambridge and Budapest, but also to those from Ado-Ekiti and Owerri.

• 6 •

Relating Africa and the Old Testament on the Polygamy Issue

The task of relating Africa and the Old Testament on the polygamy issue can be approached from different points of view.[1] From a pastoral or practical theological point of view, one could discuss how the churches can let the Old Testament play a role in the counselling of polygamous families.[2] And, from a historical point of view, one could follow the continuous discussion within the churches with regard to the polygamy issue, and the role played by the Old Testament in this discussion.[3]

---

[1]   Paper read at the 8th Congress of the Panafrican Association of Catholic Exegetes, Ouagadougou, Burkina Faso, July 1997; the major theme of the congress was "Church as family: Biblical perspectives". Polygamy is the possession of more than one spouse at a time, either as polygyny: marriage with more than one wife, or as polyandry: marriage with more than one man; however, as it occurs almost only in the form of polygyny, the term polygamy is here used as a synonym for the term polygyny.

[2]   Cf. e.g. W. Trobisch, *My wife made me a polygamist* (1967).

[3]   It should here be noted that some of the previous missionary reluctance to translate the Old Testament into African languages was probably due to the fear that certain Old Testament narratives might be "misused" to propagate polygamy, and thereby

However, rather than discussing pastoral or historical questions, this paper will focus on some methodological questions. When two completely different entities such as "Africa" and "the Old Testament" are being related, for example on the polygamy issue, it is important that we occasionally stop and ask some basic how- and why-questions. And that is what I will do in the following; in two steps: First, brief presentations of the institutions of polygamy in Africa and in the Old Testament, *per se*. And then the major focus of the paper, a discussion of how and why we relate these two institutions to each other.

Polygamy in Africa

Throughout Africa the institution of polygamy has been, and, in some contexts still is, looked upon as a traditional ideal. Still, even where it is practised, polygamy is realised only by a minority of men, at least at the same time. In his famous book *Polygamy reconsidered* (1975), Eugene Hillman emphasises that "[...] monogamous unions actually outnumber polygamous ones".[4] However, in principle, there is no fundamental difference between the two; generally speaking, the extent of polygamy depends on the status of the husband. Those who can afford to have several wives do so, partly because of the benefits of more labour and more children, but partly also as a mark of high position. Hillman therefore continues that "[...] monogamous unions will usually tend to be potentially polygamous."

How, then, should this institution be interpreted? One could hardly say that polygamy as such has been a central topic in the history of anthropological studies of Africa. Still, as it touches other topics that have been more popular among anthropologists, such as kinship studies and, more recently, women studies, polygamy has gained at least some attention. Let me, very briefly, give two glimpses into this area of anthropological research.

The first glimpse is from the colonial period, where the so-called British school of anthropology showed a strong interest for kinship

---

cause secession from the historical churches. As for the indigenous churches, which have often been quite open towards traditional marriage patterns, it is pointed out by D.B. Barrett, *Schism and renewal in Africa* (1968) 116–119, that polygamy has been the immediate cause of secession only in a very few cases.

4   E. Hillman, *Polygamy reconsidered* (1975) 88.

studies. For an Old Testament scholar the obvious example (cf. below) is of course Edward E. Evans-Pritchard, who in his studies of the Nilotic Nuer occasionally visits also the institution of polygamy. Evans-Pritchard is especially interested in the function of this institution within the marriage and kinship patterns of the Nuer. He notices that a man's wives have an equal status, and that arrangements are being made to strengthen the ties between them. Thus, according to Evans-Pritchard, polygamy "[...] is for the Nuer the ideal form of family life and every man would like to attain to it."[5] Similar observations are also reflected in the publications of many of his contemporaries; see for example several of the papers in the collection edited by Alfred R. Radcliffe-Brown and Daryll Forde in 1950, entitled *African systems of kinship and marriage.*[6] Characteristic of the research of this generation was a preference for what the American anthropologist Sally Falk Moore has recently called a production of "[...] 'pure' editions of the cultures they were describing"; in other words, they were interested in "[...] how these societies 'functioned' before the colonial intervention."[7]

The second glimpse into this area of anthropological research is from the postcolonial period, where anthropologists from different scholarly angles have focused on woman studies, and thereby also touched the institution of polygamy. The Ugandan anthropologist Christine Obbo, in her book *African women: Their struggle for economic independence* (1980), has emphasised that changing socio-economic conditions strongly affect the lives and roles of African women. One consequence of the material pleasures of a westernised life style caused by urbanisation and industrialisation, is that fewer men can afford to support more than one wife. So, according to Obbo, the practice of polygamy is nowadays curbed, not so much by laws or religious dogma on monogamy, but rather by the demands for shoes and skirts of the latest fashion![8] However, changing socio-economic conditions could also influence the institution of polygamy in other directions. Kenneth Little, in his book *African women in towns* (1973), has noticed that a consequence of the economic emancipation of women in some South

5   E.E. Evans-Pritchard, *Kinship and marriage among the Nuer* (1951) 124–151, 140.

6   A.R. Radcliffe-Brown & D. Forde, *African systems of kinship and marriage* (1950); cf. e.g. M. Fortes, "Kinship and marriage among the Ashanti", pp. 252–284.

7   S.F. Moore, *Anthropology and Africa* (1994) 23–24.

8   C. Obbo, *African women* (1980) 97, 33–53.

African townships, is that some sort of a disguised polygamy seem to
reoccur; here, however, not only as polygyny, but even as polyandry.[9]
Thus, both Obbo and Little, and also a number of other anthropologists,
for example several of those represented in David Parkin & David
Nyamwaya's *Transformations of African marriage* (1987), focus on the
rapid cultural and socio-economic changes experienced by contemporary
Africa; changes that also affect the institution of polygamy.[10]

Two things should therefore be noted with regard to the
anthropological study of the institution of polygamy in Africa. First, the
approaches of the anthropologists to these phenomena are changing,
from the synchronic studies of the past, where polygamy and other so-
called "customs" were given a rather static interpretation, to the more
diachronic studies of today, where change and dynamic aspects are
emphasised. Secondly, and closely related, not only the methodology of
the anthropologists, but also the object of their studies is changing.
Urbanisation, industrialisation, and a number of other factors, for
example AIDS, create new social patterns, and this obviously has
consequences for all kinds of social structures, including marriage
patterns and thereby also the institution of polygamy.

Polygamy in the Old Testament

Turning to the Old Testament, in an attempt to figure out what it says
about polygamy, we should bear in mind that, at least till now, most
professional Old Testament interpreters have come from societies that
are unfamiliar with the institution of (at least simultaneous!) polygamy,
whereas the texts we interpret clearly reflect a society that is familiar
with this institution. This cultural difference complicates the
interpretation of the Old Testament texts, and it demonstrates the
importance of letting the Old Testament be read by new eyes, also
professionally speaking. With "new eyes" I primarily think of non-
western eyes, as the most obvious example of "new eyes" within western
Old Testament scholarship, those of feminist interpreters, hardly reflect
any attitude that is more open towards the institution of polygamy than

---

9   K. Little, *African women in towns* (1973) 106–107.

10   D. Parkin & D. Nyamwaya (eds.), *Transformations of African marriage* (1987); cf.
     e.g. R. Clignet, "On dit que la polygamie est morte: Vive la polygamie!", pp. 199–
     209.

that of the traditional "white, middle-class males"; cf. for example Alice L. Laffey, who, in her *An introduction to the Old Testament: A feminist perspective* (1988), lists polygamy as one of the phenomena in the Old Testament that "[...] testify to women's inferior role as unequal partners in a patriarchal society."[11]

When we take a closer look at the texts of the Old Testament, we find that there is a striking tension between monogamous and polygamous practices. On the one hand, the ideal marriage seems to be the monogamous one. A monogamous tradition is reflected throughout the Old Testament, from the Eden narrative in Genesis 2–3, via a number of laws (cf. e.g. Exodus 20:17), and to the Wisdom literature (cf. e.g. Proverbs 12:4, 18:22). On the other hand, however, the Old Testament also contains a number of narratives (cf. e.g. Genesis 16:1 ff., 26:34, 28:9, 29:15–30, Judges 8:30, 10:4, 12:8–9, 19:1, 1 Samuel 1:2, 25:1–44, 2 Samuel 3:2–5, 5:13, 1 Kings 11:3), and even some laws (Exodus 21:7–11, Deuteronomy 17:17, 21:15–17), reflecting a polygamous setting.

A favoured solution to this tension is that polygamy was for the top layer of society, whereas monogamy was for the huge majority. A typical example of this view is found in Roland de Vaux's *Ancient Israel: Its life and institutions*, which, in its discussion of the polygamy issue, argues that: "It is noteworthy that the books of Samuel and Kings, which cover the entire period of the monarchy, do not record a single case of bigamy among commoners (except that of Samuel's father, at the very beginning of the period)."[12] Still, against this one could, as Victor P. Hamilton has done, argue that "[...] the books of Samuel and Kings record little about any commoner, or the marriage of any commoner."[13]

Accordingly, although the tension between polygamy and monogamy in the Old Testament has received much attention from historical critical scholars,[14] there is still a lot to be done; with regard to the exegetical relationship within the different traditions of the Old

---

[11] A.L. Laffey, *An introduction to the Old Testament* (1988) 18.

[12] R. de Vaux, *Ancient Israel* (1984) 25.

[13] V.P. Hamilton, "Marriage: Old Testament and Ancient Near East", *The Anchor Bible Dictionary* 4 (1992) 565.

[14] For surveys of relevant literature, cf. e.g. V.P. Hamilton, "Marriage: Old Testament and Ancient Near East", *The Anchor Bible Dictionary* 4 (1992) 568–569; K. Engelken, "פלגש", *Theologisches Wörterbuch zum Alten Testament* 6 (1989) 586; T. Kronholm, "Polygami och monogami i Gamla testamentet", *Svensk Exegetisk Årsbok* 47 (1982) 48–49.

Testament as well as with regard to the relationship between the
marriage patterns of the Old Testament and those of the Ancient Near
East.

Polygamy in Africa related to polygamy in the Old Testament

Now, having surveyed polygamy in Africa and polygamy in the Old
Testament, and how these two historically and geographically separated
institutions can be interpreted, we should move on, and relate the two to
each other.

We are certainly not the first ones to do this. A number of African
theologians and exegetes, and even some non-Africans, have in recent
years commented upon the relationship between Africa and the Old
Testament on the polygamy issue. However, it is my impression that in
most cases this is done without showing any explicit awareness of the
methodological questions which arise when we relate phenomena of a
contemporary culture, to which we have access through field studies and
personal experience, to similar phenomena of a culture of the past, to
which we have access only through some few and scattered references in
ancient written sources. There is, accordingly, a need for some
methodological reflection on the relationship between Africa and the Old
Testament with regard to the polygamy issue. And that is what I will
attempt to do in the following; in two steps, first a brief presentation of
three articles where polygamy in Africa and in the Old Testament are
being related, and then a discussion of two basic approaches that are
reflected in these three, and other, examples.

Three examples
The three examples to be presented should be quite representative of how
Africa and the Old Testament have been related on the polygamy issue in
recent years, as they cover three decades (the 1970s, 80s and 90s) and
three parts of the continent (South, West and East Africa).

The first example is taken from an article entitled "Some African
insights and the Old Testament", published by the well known South
African theologian and church leader Desmond Tutu in *Journal of
Theology for Southern Africa* as early as 1972. Tutu here seeks to
demonstrate that Old Testament readers acquainted with traditional
African culture have a more direct access to the texts than, say, western
readers. According to Tutu, "[...] the Biblical world view in many ways

is far more congenial for the African than for western man—the African is much more on the wave length of the Bible than western man was originally."[15] Thus, when Tutu reads the Old Testament, his own African experience is used as a key to the culture that is reflected in the texts.

One of Tutu's examples of this African insight into the Old Testament is the polygamy issue. Tutu points out that polygamy in traditional Africa hardly reflects a promiscuous nature of man; its function is rather to secure male children, to carry on the name of the father. And, according to Tutu, this is also the case in the Old Testament. In other words, by reading the Old Testament texts on polygamy in the light of an African understanding of polygamy, Tutu claims to be able to add new insights into the interpretation of the Old Testament.[16]

The second example is taken from the article "Toward a biblical understanding of polygamy", published in the journal *Missiology* in 1989 by the American missionary Pamela S. Mann.[17] Her context is the Lutheran church in Cameroon, and its continuous struggle with the polygamy issue. From within this context, where she experiences a strong need among the grassroots members of the church for a redefinition of the attitude of the church towards polygamy, she approaches the Scriptures, ironically admitting that both American and Cameroonian readers would be outraged by her views on polygamy.[18]

Mann lists all the Old Testament polygamists, noting what she calls the "effect" of the polygamy, that is how it is evaluated by the biblical authors. Of a total number of 19 cases of polygamy in the Old Testament, five are argued to have a positive effect; these five cases include Lamech, whose two wives gave birth to the two creative children Jubal and Tubal-Cain (Genesis 4:19–22); Esau, who married a third and, according to Mann, "God-fearing wife" (Genesis 28:8–9); David, whose wives are reckoned by Nathan as God's blessing (2 Samuel 12:8); Abijah, who, with his fourteen wives, was preferred over Jeroboam by God (2 Chronicles 13:21); and finally Joash, who "[...] did what was

---

15   D. Tutu, "Some African insights and the Old Testament", *Journal of Theology for Southern Africa* 1 (1972) 19.

16   *Ibid.*, 21.

17   P.S. Mann, "Toward a biblical understanding of polygamy", *Missiology* 17 (1989) 11–26.

18   *Ibid.*, 24.

right in the eyes of the Lord all the years of Jehoiada the priest"—that is the very same priest who gave Joash two wives (2 Chronicles 24:2–3).[19]

In other words, there is, according to Mann, enough textual evidence to argue that the Old Testament does not forbid polygamy; and, it should be added, she argues that neither does the New Testament.[20] On the contrary, she claims, the Old Testament gives positive guidelines for polygamy, guidelines that should be of relevance also within the church in Cameroon; of special importance here is the right of the first wife (Exodus 21:10), and the right of the firstborn, regardless of which wife is the mother (Deuteronomy 21:15–17).

The third example, also chronologically speaking, is taken from the article "Interpreting Old Testament polygamy through African eyes", published in 1992 by the Kenyan theologian Musambi R.A. Kanyoro, in a book she co-edited with Mercy A. Oduyoye, *The will to arise: Women, tradition and the church in Africa*.[21] In this article Kanyoro discusses questions related to the translation of Old Testament texts on polygamy, proceeding from the correct observation that it is "[...] almost impossible to translate or interpret a text without coloring it, sieving it, or molding it through our own entire network of beliefs, reality and language."[22] Her method is to study the terminology used in the Hebrew texts, and then examine how Africans, who read these texts through translations into their own languages, understand this terminology in relation to African polygamy.

Kanyoro focuses on the relationship between wife and concubine, noting two sets of difficulties for the Bible translator. First, a survey of the marriage patterns that are reflected in the Old Testament shows that the exegetical relationship between these two central actors is rather difficult to define; the texts are actually quite ambiguous. Secondly, however, the Bible translator faces problems not only with the text; even the context might be difficult, as the concept of concubinage is completely foreign in some polygamous societies in Africa. These two sets of difficulties result in a wide variety of how the word "concubine"

---

[19]   *Ibid.*, 16–17; in addition to these five comes a sixth case which is considered both positive and negative.

[20]   *Ibid.*, 18–23.

[21]   M.R.A. Kanyoro, "Interpreting Old Testament polygamy through African eyes", M.A. Oduyoye & M.R.A. Kanyoro (eds.), *The will to arise* (1992) 87–100.

[22]   *Ibid.*, 87.

is translated. Kanyoro has surveyed sixteen East African translations, and she found that it is rendered as everything from "woman", "second wife", or "house servant", to "secret lover" or "sex tutor".[23] The meaning of the Old Testament texts on polygamy, according to Kanyoro, is dependent upon the values of the translators, who traditionally have been men. And, as a conclusion, she therefore points out the need for women in translation work, including women who know what it is like to be a concubine, so that their thought system can also be reflected in the translations.[24]

Two approaches
Having presented these three examples of how Africa and the Old Testament are being related on the polygamy issue, I will proceed to the question of methodology, and discuss some of the exegetical and hermeneutical questions that are reflected in these and other examples.

I believe Africa and the Old Testament are being related on the polygamy issue for mainly two very different reasons; different with respect to which of the two is used to interpret which. On the one hand, Africa can be used to interpret the Old Testament; that is, the African experience of polygamy can be used as comparative material in exegetical analyses of Old Testament texts on polygamy. On the other hand, the Old Testament can be used to interpret Africa; that is, the Old Testament texts on polygamy can be used in hermeneutical studies of the relevance of the Old Testament to its contemporary African readers. It should be admitted that this distinction between an exegetical approach, where the African experience provides some help for the interpretation of the Old Testament, and a hermeneutical approach, where the Old Testament provide some help for the interpretation of the lives of its contemporary African readers, is seldom reflected explicitly in the current literature on the relationship between Africa and the Old Testament on the polygamy issue, including the three articles just presented. Still, as this distinction provides some tools for a clearer understanding of how we can relate Africa and the Old Testament, and obviously also why we do it, I believe that it, methodologically speaking, is important to distinguish between the two.

---

23   *Ibid.*, 97.
24   *Ibid.*, 99.

Let us start with the approach that uses comparative material from Africa in exegetical analyses of the Old Testament. The basic idea here is that affinities and parallels exist, somehow, between the religio-cultural tradition of Africa and the religion and culture that is reflected in the Old Testament.[25] Edward E. Evans-Pritchard is often quoted for having pointed out that the Nuer "[...] have features which bring to mind the Hebrews of the Old Testament"; he also refers to a missionary who said that she felt as if she "[...] were living in Old Testament times".[26] But Evans-Pritchard was not the first to find striking parallels between Africa and the Old Testament, nor was he the last.

In recent years, the relationship between Old Testament scholarship and anthropology, including anthropological studies of Africa, has been described by several scholars; for surveys, see general introductions, as those by John W. Rogerson, *Anthropology and the Old Testament* (1978), and Thomas W. Overholt, *Cultural anthropology and the Old Testament* (1996),[27] and collections of essential essays, as those edited by Berhard Lang, *Anthropological approaches to the Old Testament* (1985), and Charles E. Carter & Carol E. Meyers, *Community, identity, and ideology: Social science approaches to the Hebrew Bible* (1996).[28] These contributions point out the difficulties and pitfalls facing anyone who wants to draw lines between the Old Testament and religion and culture of a contemporary society; however, they also show some of the challenges and possibilities.

With regard to difficulties and pitfalls, the major problem with most attempts at relating Africa and the Old Testament on the polygamy issue, is that it is being done at a superficial level. The very fact that polygamy exists as a social institution in Africa, and that a corresponding institution is reflected also in the Old Testament, has too often led scholars to draw superficial lines between the two. One example could

---

25   It is, of course, also possible to discuss the African patterns of polygamy in the light of biblical and Christian ethical teaching *without* relating affinities and parallels between the African and the Old Testament expressions of polygamy; this is the case both with E. Hillman's *Polygamy reconsidered* (1975), and W.G. Blum's counter-book *Forms of marriage: Monogamy reconsidered* (1989).

26   E.E. Evans-Pritchard, *Nuer religion* (1970) vii.

27   J.W. Rogerson, *Anthropology and the Old Testament* (1978); T.W. Overholt, *Cultural anthropology and the Old Testament* (1996).

28   B. Lang (ed.), *Anthropological approaches to the Old Testament* (1985); C.E. Carter & C.L. Meyers (eds.), *Community, identity, and ideology* (1996).

be the article referred to above by Desmond Tutu, where apparently casual aspects of polygamy in Africa are related to just as casual aspects of polygamy referred to by the Old Testament. Somewhat better is a study published by the Nigerian Old Testament scholar Gabriel O. Abe in 1989; a study relating the social institutions of marriage, including polygamous marriage, in the Old Testament and among the Yoruba of Nigeria.[29] Abe here makes use of both exegetical and anthropological literature; still, even this study suffers from a lack of methodological awareness of the difference between exegetical and anthropological data. As exegetes we take for granted that any study involving Old Testament texts should be methodologically well founded. However, it should be obvious that the same must be the case also with regard to the anthropological components of the study. David Fiensy has surveyed how the insight provided by Evans-Pritchard and other anthropologists on the Nuer culture has been used by Old Testament scholars as a key into the ancient Israelite culture reflected in the Old Testament. And he is certainly right when he points out the necessity for Old Testament scholars of being sensitive to the current methodological debate in the field of anthropology, in order to ensure that biblical research is not based on discredited theories.[30]

However, the task of relating Africa and the Old Testament does not offer only difficulties and pitfalls. There are indeed also challenges and possibilities waiting for the one who wants to use African comparative material in the interpretation of the Old Testament. Not least Thomas W. Overholt has emphasised and exemplified that cross-cultural comparison can be used fruitfully in the study of the Old Testament,[31] and I am sure that this also concerns the polygamy question.

In my opinion, commentators such as Desmond Tutu and Gabriel O. Abe are basically right when they assume that some affinities and parallels exist between Africa and the Old Testament on the polygamy issue. In that regard it is interesting to note that Pamela Mann points out that some of the texts which western interpreters traditionally have taken to imply monogamy, could also be interpreted otherwise. For example,

---

29   G.O. Abe, "The Jewish and Yoruba social institution of marriage", *Orita* 21/I (1989) 3–18.

30   D. Fiensy, "Using the Nuer culture of Africa in understanding the Old Testament", *Journal for the Study of the Old Testament* 38 (1987) 73–83.

31   Cf. T.W. Overholt, *Cultural anthropology* (1996) 13–17; for a broader discussion, cf. his *Prophecy in a cross-cultural perspective* (1986).

with regard to the "one flesh" in Genesis 2:24, she points out that from an African point of view, "A decent polygamist [...] can be one flesh with the first wife on her day of cooking and sleeping with him and then one flesh with his second wife on her day."[32]

Accordingly, I believe that some of the anthropological data on the social function of polygamy in Africa can be used fruitfully in the exegetical interpretation of Old Testament texts on polygamy; and then, not only data from synchronic studies within traditional and supposedly "independent units", but also data from diachronic studies, providing models for cultural change. The challenge for the Old Testament scholar, however, is to use the data in a way that takes account of both exegetical and anthropological methodology.

The second approach to the task of relating Africa and the Old Testament on the polygamy issue is to let the Old Testament provide some help for the interpretation of the lives of its contemporary African readers, of whom at least some live in polygamous marriages.

African theology is often characterised by the key words inculturation and liberation.[33] The hermeneutical approaches referred to by these two key words are also, to some degree, reflected in African Old Testament scholarship; the inculturation hermeneutical approach focuses on an interpretation of the Old Testament that has its roots firmly planted in African culture and traditions, whereas the liberation hermeneutical approach focuses on an interpretation of the Old Testament that acknowledges God's liberative activity from any oppression based on politics, economy, race, or gender.

These two approaches are also relevant in our discussion of the relationship between Africa and the Old Testament on the polygamy issue. From an inculturation hermeneutical point of view, the Old Testament references to polygamous families and to polygamy as an institution can be used to draw lines between the Old Testament and the lives of its contemporary African readers. This aspect is, for example, reflected in the article by Gabriel O. Abe, referred to above, and in an article from 1983 by Emmanuel I. Ifesieh.[34] It also plays a major role in

---

[32]   P.S. Mann, "Toward a biblical understanding of polygamy", *Missiology* 17 (1989) 15.

[33]   Cf. E. Martey, *African theology* (1993).

[34]   E.I. Ifesieh, "Web of matrimony in the Bible, social anthropology and African traditional religion", *Communio Viatorum* 26 (1983) 195–211.

Pamela Mann's article, and the question posed by Mann is this: "Can the Scriptures provide a marriage model which is both spiritually sound and thoroughly African?"[35] Her answer is affirmative. She emphasises that the expression "thoroughly African" includes marriage models where polygamy is a customary option; the crucial point is that even the "[...] African polygamist must be faithful in his marriage agreement with his wives."

But also a liberation hermeneutical approach can offer a relevant reading of the Old Testament references to polygamy. Several women theologians in Africa have pointed out that aspects of traditional African culture that are negative toward women can be reinforced by the Old Testament. Mercy A. Oduyoye, for example, has pointed out that that there is a correspondence between the traditional oppression of women in Africa and the oppression of women reflected in the Old Testament.[36] Now, polygamy as such does not necessarily reflect any oppression of women. However, within polygamous contexts, as within monogamous contexts, there are examples of oppression. And here some Old Testament texts on polygamy can have a liberating function. One aspect is noted by Pamela Mann, when she points out that texts like Deuteronomy 17:17 and Exodus 21:10 emphasise that the polygamous husband should limit the number of wives and treat his wives in the same way.[37] Another aspect is noted by Musambi Kanyoro, when she uses the relationship between polygamy in Africa and in the Old Testament to advocate the need for women translators of the Bible in Africa: "[...] unless women also get into the area of Bible translation, the thought system of women will remain unreflected in the text we receive. The language of the Bible will also remain masculine until the women take up the will to rise and influence this aspect of the Christian's base."[38]

---

35   P.S. Mann, "Toward a biblical understanding of polygamy", *Missiology* 17 (1989) 14.

36   M.A. Oduyoye, "Naming the woman", *Bulletin of African Theology* 3 (1985) 81–97; for a survey of other studies, cf. L. Lagerwerf, "African women doing theology", *Exchange* 19 (1990) 30–35.

37   P.S. Mann, "Toward a biblical understanding of polygamy", *Missiology* 17 (1989) 17, 25.

38   M.R.A. Kanyoro, "Interpreting Old Testament polygamy through African eyes", M.A. Oduyoye & M.R.A. Kanyoro (eds.), *The will to arise* (1992) 99.

Concluding remarks

In this paper I have focused on methodological questions. I have pointed out the importance of knowing and distinguishing between some of the how's and why's that come up when we relate Africa and the Old Testament on the polygamy issue.

By this focus on methodology I do not want to be understood as if I am neglecting all the other aspects of the relationship between Africa and the Old Testament on the polygamy issue. Let me therefore emphasise that I clearly see the complexity of this issue; a complexity where all exegetical and hermeneutical discussion first of all should bear in mind that the object of our discussion, "the polygamy issue", touches existential questions of people living in polygamous marriages, that is, it touches the lives of human beings of flesh and blood.

Still, as all readers of the Old Testament read the texts in the light of their own context, it is important that we try to explore some the how's and why's of the relationship between ancient text and reader's context. And in an African context that includes the relationship between Africa and the Old Testament on the polygamy issue.

Africa in the Old Testament

• 7 •

Africa in the Old Testament

Africa in the Old Testament (OT): to many OT readers, in Africa as well as outside, this topic may sound rather exotic; few have thought of the idea that the ancient texts of the OT have anything to say about Africa. However, to other readers, mainly in Africa or in the African diaspora, this topic touches existential questions; the place of Africa in the OT is related to their identity as well as their history. Accordingly, whether the topic Africa in the OT is seen as exotic or existential, depends on the eyes that see. The present essay acknowledges this and takes sides; it is consciously written from the perspective that a closer study of what the ancient texts of the OT say about Africa is of importance for its contemporary African readers.

The presentation and discussion of the topic Africa in the OT will be done in three steps. First, an introductory section, which aims to clarify some definitions and the background and material of this enterprise. Then follows the major section, which makes a textual survey of how some African nations and even some African individuals are portrayed throughout the OT. And finally, a brief summary of the findings, noting some hermeneutical questions.

Definitions and material

Let us start with a definition of the two terms "OT" and "Africa". First, while the term "OT" may seem relatively unproblematic (except to those who would prefer the designation "Hebrew Bible", though this is seldom used in Africa), referring in the minds of most scholars to the Masoretic canon, this understanding is not without problems, as no less than two broader canons, competing with the Masoretic one, have their background in Africa: the Alexandrian and the Ethiopian. Just what constitutes the "OT" has been problematised, and some have argued that African translations of the OT, and hence also African interpretations of the OT, should follow the broader African canons.[1] I raise this concern, but will not develop it. My focus is on the second term, "Africa"; the term "Africa" usually designates the African continent. But this understanding is not without difficulties as well. One is what we are to do with Egypt: is it appropriate to say that ancient Egypt was an African nation; would it not be more accurate to say that it belonged to the Ancient Near East? Another related problem is what to do with the areas surrounding the Red Sea: is it appropriate to distinguish between an African and an Arabian side;[2] is it not so that such a distinction just demonstrates the problems of approaching ancient sources with modern geographical and cartographic concepts? Some of these problems we will come back to. Still, in this essay "Africa" refers to the African continent.

Only a brief glance into the current scholarly literature on the OT is enough to realise that traditional western OT scholarship has not shown much interest in the portrayal of Africa in the OT. On the contrary, western literature on the OT, from Bible atlases and histories of Israel to dictionaries and commentaries, has been accused of reflecting a more or less deliberate de-Africanisation. African nations such as Egypt and even Cush, it has been argued, are either located in the so-called Ancient Near East rather than in Africa, or their cultural influence on ancient Israel is neglected.[3] However, the picture is probably somewhat more complex.

---

1   Cf. S.P. Kealy, "The canon: An African contribution", *Biblical Theology Bulletin* 9 (1979) 13–26.

2   Cf. G.L. Yorke, "Biblical hermeneutics: An Afrocentric perspective", *Religion & Theology* 2 (1995) 150.

3   Cf. R.C., Bailey, "Beyond identification", C.H. Felder (ed.), *Stony the road we trod* (1991) 165–168.

Some of the western reluctance might be an understandable reaction to sometimes fanciful attempts in earlier times at drawing lines between Africa and the OT, for example the identification in the late 19th century of the newly discovered wealth of Zimbabwe with OT Ophir.[4] However, several western OT scholars have actually shown some interest in drawing lines between Africa and the OT, in a few cases this was directly due to their encounter with the African interest in this topic.[5] Still, it should be admitted that the quest for an analysis of the OT portrayal of Africa has not been, and still not is, regarded as a priority within traditional western OT scholarship.

However, within parts of African and African American OT scholarship the situation is quite the opposite; though with some terminological (and ideological) differences. Whereas the former tends to talk about an African presence in the OT, the latter tends to talk about a black presence. Whatever this presence is called, attempts at giving it a scholarly description have been made from the early 1970s and throughout the 1980s and 90s by Africans such as Engelbert Mveng and David T. Adamo, and African Americans such as Robert A. Bennet and Charles B. Copher and Alvin A. Jackson.[6] Of special importance here is the contribution made by the Nigerian scholar David T. Adamo; in a number of studies he has focused on the OT references to Cush, arguing that these reflect close connections between ancient Israel and Africa.[7]

Adamo's focus on Cush demonstrates the need for a clarification of which geographical entities referred to by the OT can, with some certainty, be located to the continent of Africa. This is necessary in order to define the relevant material for the present study of the OT portrayal of Africa. The relevant geographical entities can be grouped into three

---

4   Cf. R. North, "Ophir/Parvaim and Petra/Joktheel", *Proceedings of the World Congress of Jewish Studies* 4 (1967) 200.

5   Cf. R.W. Anderson, "Zephaniah ben Cushi and Cush of Benjamin", S.W Holloway & L.K. Handy (eds.), *The pitcher is broken* (1995) 45–46.

6   Cf. E. Mveng, "La bible et l'afrique noire", E. Mveng & R.Z. Werblowsky (eds.), *The Jerusalem congress* (1972) 23–39; D.T. Adamo, *Africa and the Africans in the Old Testament* (1998); R.A. Bennet, "Africa and the biblical period", *Harvard Theological Review* 64 (1971) 483–500; A.A. Jackson, *Examining the record* (1994).

7   Cf. Adamo's works listed in the bibliography, most recently his *Africa and the Africans in the Old Testament* (1998); for a critical discussion, cf. M. Høyland, "An African presence in the Old Testament?", *Old Testament Essays* 11 (1998) 50–58.

categories: those referring to Egypt, those referring to Cush, and then a number of different entities with fewer references or more uncertain location. Before I discuss each of these in detail, some comments on the relationship between the references to Egypt and Cush may be useful. From a numerical point of view the approximately 680 references to Egypt reflect a closer focus than the 56 references to Cush/Cushi (30/26).[8] Further, the proportional relationship between the two is not the same throughout the OT: the Law has 6 references to Cush and approximately 350 to Egypt, the Prophets have 33 (Former: 8, Latter: 25) to Cush and approximately 280 to Egypt (Former: 80, Latter: 200), and the Writings have 17 to Cush and approximately 50 to Egypt. However, in my search for the OT portrayal of Africa, Cush will receive an attention equal to that of Egypt, for two reasons. First, the OT portrayal of Cush echoes aspects of Africa and Africans that go beyond the geographical, cultural, and anthropological borders of Egypt and further into Africa. Secondly, African and African American scholars, in their search for Africa in the OT, have focused so strongly on Cush as a representative for Africa.

Egypt

Let us then proceed to the textual survey, searching for the OT portrayal of the three groups pointed out above. We will start with Egypt, whose location in the north-eastern corner of the African continent made it a bridge, both geographically and culturally, between the Ancient Near East and Africa. Traditionally, scholars have emphasised the relationship between Egypt and the Ancient Near East. In recent years, however, one has become increasingly aware of its African heritage. On the one hand, the geographical source for the peopling of the Egyptian Nile Valley seems to have been predominantly African, rather than European or Near Eastern,[9] and, on the other hand, the civilisation formed here was "[...] to an extent usually not recognised, fundamentally African. The evidence of

---

8   For a survey of the references, cf. A. Even-Shoshan, *A new concordance of the Old Testament* (1993) 700–703 (for Egypt) and 527 (for Cush).

9   Cf. S.O.Y. Keita, "Studies and comments on ancient Egyptian biological relationships", *History of Africa* 20 (1993) 129–154.

both language and culture reveals these African roots."[10] Also ancient Israel had a long history of contact with its mighty neighbour in the south;[11] the approximately 680 references to Egypt in the OT vividly demonstrate this contact.[12] Still, in the African and African American search for the portrayal of Africa in the OT, the traditions related to Egypt have only occasionally been included.[13] This is mainly due to a definition of Africa that emphasises "[...] the area inhabited by black Africans in the south of the Sahara",[14] rather than the African continent as a whole, as is the case in this essay.

Starting with the pentateuchal portrayal of Egypt, we find that it is linked, first and foremost, to the traditions of Israel's sojourn in what is called "the land of slavery" (see Exodus 13:3) or "the iron-smelting furnace" (see Deuteronomy 4:20). These expressions reflect central aspects of the narrative traditions about the experiences in Egypt; negatively, the traditions emphasise the experience of suffering and humiliation (see Exodus 1–11), and positively, they locate the experience of suffering and struggle as the background for the experience of Yahweh's salvation (see Exodus 12–14). The importance of these traditions is also seen in that they are reflected in central pentateuchal creeds and formulas. The creed in Deuteronomy 26:5–10 presents the Egyptians as the ones who "[...] ill-treated us and made us suffer, putting us to hard labour" (v. 6); the Deuteronomy variant of the Sabbath commandment reminds Israel that "[...] you were slaves in Egypt" (Deuteronomy 5:15), and both variants of the Decalogue presents

---

10   C. Ehret, "Ancient Egyptian as an African language, Egypt as an African culture", T. Celenko (ed.), *Egypt in Africa* (1996) 25.

11   For a survey, cf. R.J. Williams, "II. Ägypten und Israel", *Theologische Realenzyklopädie* 1 (1977) 492–505.

12   Cf. G. Pfeifer, *Ägypten im Alten Testament* (1995); a recent contribution that probably goes too far in emphasising the historicity of the literary portrayal of the OT with regard to this contact, is J.D. Currid, *Ancient Egypt and the Old Testament* (1997).

13   Cf. R.A. Bennet, "Africa and the biblical period", *Harvard Theological Review* 64 (1971) 483–500; C.B. Copher, *Black biblical studies* (1993) 45–65.

14   D.T. Adamo, *The place of Africa* (1986) 5; cf. also E. Mveng, "La bible et l'afrique noire", E. Mveng & R.Z. Werblowsky (eds.), *The Jerusalem congress* (1972) 23–39; and S. Sempore, "Le noir et le salut dans la bible", P. Adeso & al. (eds.), *Universalisme et mission dans la bible* (1993) 17–29.

Yahweh as the one who "[...] brought you out of Egypt, out of the land of slavery" (Exodus 20:2, Deuteronomy 5:6).

A closer study of the Pentateuch shows a number of more positive portrayals of Egypt. One aspect of this is Egypt as an asylum for refugees who had to flee Israel due to famine or political problems.[15] This image of Egypt frequently comes up in the patriarchal narratives. Abraham went down to Egypt due to a famine in Canaan (Genesis 12:10), and during another famine Isaac needed a special command from Yahweh not to seek help in Egypt (Genesis 26:2). Joseph collected food throughout seven years of abundance in Egypt (Genesis 41:41–57), and thereby not only the Egyptians, but also Jacob and his family survived still another famine. A closely related aspect is the richness and fertility of Egypt. Egypt can be likened to the garden of Eden (Genesis 13:10), and it constitutes the background for the growth of the people of Israel; seventy descendants of Jacob went down to Egypt, but eventually they "[...] were fruitful and multiplied greatly and became exceedingly numerous, so that the land was filled with them" (Exodus 1:5–7). After their departure from Egypt, Israel could therefore look back with longer for, not only the "pots of meat" (Exodus 16:2), but also to the "[...] cucumbers, melons, leeks, onions and garlic" (Numbers 11:5).

These positive aspects of the portrayal of Egypt are also reflected elsewhere in narrative and legislative pentateuchal texts. A mixed marriage between an Egyptian and an Israelite can, for instance, be mentioned without any condemnation (Leviticus 24:10–16). And whereas Ammonites and Moabites were never to be admitted into the congregation of Yahweh, not even after ten generations, Egyptians could do so after only three generations (Deuteronomy 23:4–9).

Turning to the Prophets, we notice that the references to Egypt in the Former Prophets (Joshua, Judges, Samuel, Kings) express some of the same tension attested already in the Pentateuch. On the one hand, Egypt is the place of suffering and humiliation (see e.g. 1 Samuel 10:18), from which Israel was freed by Yahweh (cf. e.g. Joshua 24:5). On the other hand, however, Egypt continues to be an asylum for political refugees from Israel (see e.g. 1 Kings 11:40, 2 Kings 25:26), and eventually it can even be a coalition partner for the king in Jerusalem (see e.g. 2 Kings 18:21.24). Also the Latter Prophets (Isaiah, Jeremiah, Ezekiel, the twelve minor prophets) let Egypt play several roles. Of special importance are

---

15   Cf. M. Cogan, "The other Egypt", M.V. Fox & al. (eds.), *Texts, temples, and tradition* (1996) 65–70.

the so-called oracles against the nations. Isaiah warns against making an alliance with Egypt (see Isaiah 20 and 30:1–5), arguing that "[...] the Egyptians are men and not God, and their horses are flesh and not spirit" (Isaiah 31:1–3, v. 3). Jeremiah pronounces judgement over Egypt, describing the defeat of Pharaoh Neco (Jeremiah 46:2–12) and the attack by Nebuchadnezzar (Jeremiah 46:14–28). And Ezekiel likens Egypt to a sea monster (Ezekiel 29) or a cedar (Ezekiel 31); the sea monster will be left in the desert, the cedar will be cut down, and Egypt will be judged by Yahweh (Ezekiel 30). Still, in the midst of all this judgement, Isaiah 19 foresees a time of blessing, when Israel is Yahweh's inheritance and Egypt is his people (cf. v. 25).

Finally, there are some references to Egypt also in the Writings (Psalms, Job, Proverbs, Ruth, Song of Songs, Ecclesiastes, Lamentations, Esther, Daniel, Ezra, Nehemiah, Chronicles). Egypt can positively be portrayed as bringing gifts to Jerusalem (see Psalms 68:32 [ET 31]), and negatively it will experience Yahweh's judgement (see Daniel 11:42). However, the majority of the references to Egypt focus on the traditions about the sojourn and exodus, both in the Psalms (see Psalms 81:6.11, 105:23.38, 114:1, 135:8–9, 136:10) and elsewhere (see Daniel 9:15, 2 Chronicles 6:5, 7:22, Nehemiah 9:9 ff.).

Cush

The OT is also aware of a nation that is located south of Egypt (cf. Ezekiel 29:10); a nation called Cush by the OT. In most cases (see below) OT Cush seems to be referring to a nation known as Kush in Ancient Near Eastern sources, and as Ethiopia in Graeco-Roman sources. This African nation was situated south of Egypt, its heartland was the area between the first and sixth cataracts of the Nile. Throughout the third and second millennia B.C. there were close connections between these areas and the mighty northern neighbour.[16] The nature of this relationship has traditionally been seen from the perspective of a superior Egyptian culture and political system; ancient Kush has to some extent been overshadowed by the impressive and better known history and culture of ancient Egypt. However, recently it has been argued that Kush

---

16   For general surveys, cf. B. Trigger, *Nubia under the Pharaohs* (1976) and W. Adams, *Nubia: Corridor to Africa* (1977).

and Egypt instead should be seen as more equal rivals, "[...] two major powers competing for resources and lands of the Lower Nile."[17]

More important for my essay is the history of Kush in the first millennium B.C. From the mid-eighth to the mid-seventh centuries B.C. Kushites controlled Egypt (the 25th, so-called Kushite dynasty), and they established a kingdom stretching from central north-east Africa to the Red Sea in the east and the Mediterranean in the north. This climax in the history of Kush is important to us, as it chronologically comes just prior to the period that saw the genesis of most of the OT. One should therefore expect that this military and political apex of Kush is reflected in the OT portrayal of Cush.

It should here be emphasised that not all 56 OT references to Cush necessarily refer to the African nation, or to individual members of that nation; some may refer, for example, to the Kassites in Babylon or to a tribal group supposed to have lived on the south-western border of Judah.[18] Still, it is clear that the majority refer to the African nation. For obvious reasons, African and African American scholars, who have been searching for the portrayal of Africa in the OT, tend to emphasise the African location of OT Cush. Adamo, for instance, argues that "Everywhere the word 'Cush' is used with a clear cut identification, it refers to Africa."[19] Adamo is also willing to go one step further; arguing that the use of Kush and Ethiopia in the extra-biblical sources refers quite broadly to black Africa, he suggests that OT Cush ought to be rendered 'Africa' in modern translations.[20]

In the Pentateuch Cush occurs already in the Eden narrative (Genesis 2–3). According to Genesis 2:10–14 four rivers were flowing out from Eden, and "The name of the second river is the Gihon; it winds through the entire land of Cush" (v. 13). The geographical location here is difficult. Gihon is the name of a spring in Jerusalem, pointing to a

---

17 Cf. D. O'Connor, *Ancient Nubia* (1993) 2.

18 Cf. S. Hidal, "The land of Cush in the Old Testament", *Svensk Exegetisk Årsbok* 41–42 (1977) 97–106; R.W. Anderson, "Zephaniah ben Cushi and Cush of Benjamin", S.W Holloway & L.K. Handy (eds.), *The pitcher is broken* (1995) 45–70; R.H. Haak, "'Cush' in Zephaniah", *ibid.* (1995) 238–251.

19 D.T. Adamo, "Ethiopia in the Bible" *African Christian Studies* 8/II (1992) 51; cf. also J.D. Hays, "The Cushites", *Bibliotheca Sacra* 153 (1996) 396–409.

20 D.T. Adamo, "Ethiopia in the Bible", *African Christian Studies* 8/II (1992) 51–64; cf. also K. Holter, "Should Old Testament Cush be rendered 'Africa'?", *The Bible Translator* 48 (1997) 331–336.

location of Eden in Israel, whereas the third and the fourth rivers are Tigris and Euphrates, pointing to a Mesopotamian location. Traditionally, many interpreters of Genesis 2 have placed also Gihon and Cush in Mesopotamia, linking Cush to the Kassites. Still, an African location is more probable.[21] There is an old tradition (cf. LXX Jeremiah 2:18; Ben Sira 24:27) of linking the name Gihon to the Nile,[22] and this allows for an interpretation of the name Cush in Genesis 2:13 in its traditional sense. This does not mean that the author of Genesis 2:10–14 actually located Eden in Africa,[23] but it means that Africa is included in the world map reflected here.[24]

Cush reoccurs twice throughout the Pentateuch. First, in the Table of nations, Genesis 10:6.7.8, Cush is mentioned first in a series of Ham's four sons; probably due to a geographical orientation starting from the far south.[25] And then, in a narrative in Numbers 12, telling about Miriam and Aaron, who criticise Moses. In the beginning of this narrative the opposition from Miriam and Aaron somehow is linked to his taking of a Cushite wife (see v. 1). This has lead some interpreters to argue that Miriam and Aaron criticise Moses for marrying a Cushite woman; this could then be taken as an example of a negative attitude towards people from Cush. However, as there are no other examples of a negative attitude in the OT towards people from Cush, this is probably not the case here either.[26] One solution is then that they criticise Moses for taking a second wife (see his marriage with Zipporah, Exodus 2:21–22), another is that the opposition from Miriam and Aaron has nothing to do with the marriage to the Cushite woman.

The eight references to Cush in the Former Prophets are found in two different narratives; both alluding to the military reputation of Cush,

---

21 Cf. the discussion in C. Westermann, *Genesis 1–11* (1974) 297–298.

22 Cf. E. Ullendorff, *Ethiopia and the Bible* (1968) 2–3.

23 So D.T. Adamo, "Ancient Africa and Genesis 2:10–14", *The Journal of Religious Thought* 49 (1992) 33–43.

24 Cf. S. Hidal, "The land of Cush in the Old Testament", *Svensk Exegetisk Årsbok* 41–42 (1977) 103–105.

25 Cf. D.T. Adamo, "The table of nations reconsidered in African perspective", *Journal of African Religion and Philosophy* 2 (1993) 138–143.

26 Cf. D.T. Adamo, "The African wife of Moses", *Africa Theological Journal* 18 (1989) 230–237; J.D. Hays, "The Cushites", *Bibliotheca Sacra* 153 (1996) 397–401.

which, historically speaking, was a result of the Cushite rule of Egypt
from the mid-eighth to the mid-seventh centuries B.C. The first narrative
is the death of Absalom, 2 Samuel 18. Here a Cushite is depicted as
serving as officer in king David's army (vv. 21–32). Interpreters of this
narrative have especially focused on how a Cushite could become an
officer in Jerusalem. Some older interpreters could, revealing their own
prejudices, present the Cushite as "[...] a negro (naturally, a slave)";[27]
however, there is nothing in the OT that supports such a view. A better
explanation is that the narrative more generally reflects a Cushite
presence in the land of Israel, that is outside the Cushite heartland.[28] An
interesting aspect of this narrative is that it lets the military skill of the
Cushites serve Israel. That is also the case in the other narrative; 2 Kings
19 depicts the Cushite king Tirhakah as a central actor in the deliverance
of Jerusalem (v. 9).

The 25 references to Cush in the Latter Prophets let Cush play
different roles. Not least is the military reputation of the Cushites
reflected several places; in lists, such as in Nahum 3:9 and Ezekiel 38:5,
or in more elaborated narratives, such as the one about Ebed-Melech the
Cushite in Jeremiah 38–39. One single verse in Amos 9 is also of
importance, due to its particular focus on the relationship between Israel
and Cush in v. 7a. Some interpreters have argued that the comparison
here of Israel with Cush expresses a judgement over Israel. A
comparison of Israel with "[...] the far-distant, uncivilised, and despised
black race of the Ethiopians",[29] it has been argued, points to a
humiliation of Israel.[30] However, the other half of the verse, v. 7b, points
in another direction. It makes a comparison that clearly is positive: the
exodus from Egypt is compared with similar experiences of other
peoples. The comparison in v. 7a ought to be interpreted in this light.[31]

---

[27]   Cf. H.P. Smith, *The Books of Samuel* (1898) 359.

[28]   Cf. R.W. Anderson, "Zephaniah ben Cushi and Cush of Benjamin", S.W Holloway
       & L.K. Handy (eds.), *The pitcher is broken* (1995) 45–70.

[29]   Cf. W.R. Harper, *A critical and exegetical commentary on Amos and Hosea* (1905)
       192.

[30]   Cf. e.g. H. Gese, "Das Problem von Amos 9,7", *Alttestamentliche Studien* (1991)
       116–121.

[31]   Cf. D.T. Adamo, "Amos 9:7–8 in an African perspective", *Orita* 24 (1992) 76–84;
       R. Smith, "A new perspective on Amos 9:7a", *Journal of the Interdenominational
       Theological Center* 22 (1994) 36–47.

The books of Isaiah and Zephaniah show a particular interest for Cush. Isaiah 18 offers the most vivid anthropological description of Cush in the OT, depicting "[...] a people tall and smooth-skinned, [...] a people feared far and wide, an aggressive nation of strange speech, whose land is divided by rivers" (v. 2); cf. also Jeremiah 13:23, quoting a proverb which asks rhetorically: "Can the Cushite change his skin or the leopard its spots?" Isaiah also alludes to the wealth of Cush (see Isaiah 43:3, 45:14)[32], seeing a time when it will bring gifts to Yahweh (see Isaiah 18:7). Still, Israel is warned against placing her trust in Cush (see Isaiah 20). When it comes to Zephaniah, already the opening verse introduces the prophet as son of Cushi (Zephaniah 1:1). Further, Cush is used to represent the far south in the prophet's geographical orientation (Zephaniah 2:4–15, v. 12); one here notices that the judgement over Cush is more briefly described than the ones of the other nations. And finally, Cush is also mentioned in a context of salvation (Zephaniah 3:10). As a whole, these references to Cush reveal a special awareness of this distant people; some interpreters argue that this reflects traces of a Cushite presence in the land of Israel,[33] whereas others have speculated more on the geographical background of Zephaniah, making him the black or African prophet of the OT.[34]

The Writings too offer examples of portrayals of Cush. One is the references in Chronicles alluding to the military reputation of Cush. Whereas Samuel and Kings let the military skill of the Cushites serve the king in Jerusalem (cf. above), the opposite is the case in Chronicles.[35] 2 Chronicles 14:8–14 [ET: 9–15] describes a war where Asa king of Judah beats Zerah the Cushite. This narrative is typical of the holy war pattern in Chronicles, as it strongly exaggerates the number of soldiers involved, and also emphasises the role played by Yahweh; cf. also 2 Chronicles 16:8 and 12:2–4.[36] Other examples of the portrayal of Cush in the

---

32   Cf. S.L. Stassen, "Die rol van Egipte, Kus en Seba in Jesaja 43:3 en 45:14", *Journal for Semitics* 4 (1992) 160–180.

33   Cf. R.W. Anderson, "Zephaniah ben Cushi and Cush of Benjamin", S.W Holloway & L.K. Handy (eds.), *The pitcher is broken* (1995) 45–70.

34   Cf. G. Rice, "The African roots of the prophet Zephaniah", *Journal of Religious Thought* 36 (1979) 21–31; D.T. Adamo, "The black prophet in the Old Testament", *Journal of Arabic and Religious Studies* 4 (1987) 1–8.

35   Cf. R.C., Bailey, "Beyond identification", C.H. Felder (ed.), *Stony the road we trod* (1991) 182.

36   Cf. J.D. Hays, "The Cushites", *Bibliotheca Sacra* 153 (1996) 401–403.

writings include Esther 1:1, which depicts the mighty Persian empire as stretching from India to Cush; Job 28:19, which alludes to the wealth of Cush; and Psalms 87:4, mentioning pilgrims from different nations, including Cush. Psalms 68:32 [ET 31] should also be mentioned here; though the text is difficult, it probably alludes to the tradition that Cush too will bring gifts to Yahweh in Jerusalem.

Other African nations

Egypt and Cush clearly offer the most relevant material in our search for Africa in the OT. Still, there is also a third group, consisting of possible Africa-linked geographical entities with few OT references and/or uncertain location.[37] Most of these are found in different kinds of lists, for example the Table of nations in Genesis 10 and 1 Chronicles 1 (see especially the descendants of Cush and Mizraim), or more scattered lists of kings or nations (see, for example Jeremiah 46:8–9, Ezekiel 30:4–5, Nahum 3:9). Some of the geographical entities have proved impossible to locate, in spite of many attempts; Ophir (see Isaiah 13:12, Job 28:16, 1 Kings 22:49) could here serve as an example.[38] Others have tentatively been located in north-east Africa or Arabia; Sabteca (Genesis 10:7, 1 Chronicles 1:9) could here serve as an example, related to Pharaoh Shebiktu or to several places in Arabia. The most relevant geographical entities can then, roughly, be grouped in two:

First, there are some which most probably have an African location; one is Put, that is Libya or Somalia (see e.g. Genesis 10:6, Nahum 3:9, Jeremiah 46:9, Ezekiel 30:5), another is Lubim, that is Libya (see e.g. 2 Chronicles 12:3, Nahum 3:9), and a third is Pathros, that is Upper Egypt (see e.g. Genesis 10:14, Jeremiah 44:15, Ezekiel 29:14). The last occurs mostly in references to the Jewish diaspora (see Isaiah 11:11, Jeremiah 44:1.14). The first two occur in lists related to war and military reputation, often together with Cush (see e.g. Nahum 3:9, Jeremiah 46:9, Ezekiel 30:5, 2 Chronicles 16:8). Lubim also has connotations of wealth, again together with Cush (cf. Daniel 11:43).

---

37   For a general survey, cf. J Simons, *The geographical and topographical texts of the Old Testament* (1959).

38   Cf. M. Görg, "Ofir und Punt", *Biblische Notizen* 82 (1996) 5–8.

Secondly, there are some locations which have ancient traditions in favour of an African location; one is Sheba, located in Africa according to Josephus, *Antiq* viii 6,5–6, another is Seba, located in Meroe, again according to Josephus, *Antiq* ii 10,2. Both have strong connotations of wealth (see e.g. Psalms 72:10.15, Ezekiel 27:22–23, Isaiah 43:3, 45:15); the latter not least due to the narrative about the Queen of Sheba (see 1 Kings 10, 2 Chronicles 9).

Conclusion

In our search for the OT portrayal of Africa, we have now been through the most relevant material. It is then time to briefly summarise our findings and relate them to some hermeneutical questions.

The textual survey can be summarised in two points. First, Africa is indeed present in the OT. Egypt and Cush, but to some extent also other African nations, play a substantial role in the OT. Egypt is the closest, geographically speaking, and consequently knowledge about Egypt and traditions about its relationship to Israel, not least the exodus tradition, are reflected throughout the OT. Cush is also well known; its location in the far south can be used to demarcate political borders, and the colour of the skin of the Cushites is used in the proverbs. Secondly, the OT reflects a dual concept of Africa, including both positive and negative lines of thought. Positively, Africa is associated with great wealth and strong military abilities; both can, at times, be used to the benefit of Israel. Negatively, however, Africa is, at other times, an enemy of Israel, oppressing and threatening her.

Both points touch important hermeneutical questions. First, they touch the question of identity. The focus on the African presence in the OT leads contemporary African readers to draw lines between their own identity and the OT portrayal of Africa. This, however, creates a hermeneutical dilemma; due to the dual concept of Africa in the OT, contemporary African readers might feel that they have to choose between the identity of the people of God or the identity of its enemies.[39] Accordingly, further hermeneutical reflection is needed. Secondly, they also touch the question of history. Traditional Eurocentric interpretation of the OT has generally marginalised the African presence in the OT.

---

[39] Cf. K. Holter, "Should Old Testament Cush be rendered 'Africa'?", *The Bible Translator* 48 (1997) 335–336.

Consequently, an Afrocentric interpretation is now challenged to reappraise the ancient OT traditions that are related to Africa, and expose contemporary OT readers to the pre-western concept of Africa reflected in these traditions.[40] Not only will this demonstrate that "Black people are not a modern-era addition to the story of salvation history. They were there from the beginning";[41] but it will also let OT scholarship contribute to "[...] the idea that Africa and persons of African descent must be seen as proactive subjects within history, rather than as passive objects of western history".[42]

40   Cf. G.L. Yorke, "Biblical hermeneutics: An Afrocentric perspective", *Religion & Theology* 2 (1995) 145–158).

41   J.D. Hays, "The Cushites: A black nation in the Bible", *Bibliotheca Sacra* 153 (1996) 409.

42   Cf. C.H. Felder, "Afrocentrism, the Bible, and the politics of difference", *Journal of Religious Thought* 50 (1993/1994) 47.

• 8 •

Should Old Testament Cush
Be Rendered 'Africa'?

A problem eventually facing any Bible translator is how to render geographical names. John A. Thompson simply answers:

> Well-known places should usually be given their modern names, not their Hebrew or Greek names.[1]

However, this approach creates new problems. What is a well-known place, and what is a modern name? Geographical names do not live their lives in a vacuum. On the contrary, they reflect their historical, political, and even ideological setting, and as such any modern name may imply connotations that are not present in its biblical predecessor. Biblical Jerusalem, for example, could probably be considered a well-known place. But what is its modern name, is it Yerushalayim or is it Al Quds?

These problems facing the modern translator are not new. The ancient translators, such as those Alexandrians responsible for the Septuagint, had to deal with similar kinds of problems. The world map of

---

[1]   J.A. Thompson, "Bible geographies and atlases and their use in translating", *The Bible Translator* 32 (1981) 431.

3rd century B.C. Alexandria was probably not the same as the world map of 6th century B.C. Jerusalem or Babylon, and, as far as geographical names are concerned, some discrepancies between the Greek and Hebrew versions of the Old Testament are therefore inevitable and understandable. It is certainly also understandable that these discrepancies are reflected in modern translations: partly because the world map of the modern translator differs from that of 3rd century B.C. Alexandria as well as that of 6th century B.C. Jerusalem or Babylon; but partly also because the modern translator finds that several of the national and political entities that are now present in what used to be Old Testament Israel, Judah, and their surroundings, have chosen ancient and ideologically pregnant names that not necessarily correspond with the names and borders of the ancient times.

The African nation Cush, which is referred to a number of times throughout the Old Testament, could be used as an illustration of some of the geographical problems facing the modern Bible translator. In the translation history of the Old Testament, from the Septuagint on, Cush has traditionally been rendered 'Ethiopia'. However, since the geographical position of the modern state of Ethiopia only marginally corresponds to that of ancient Cush, other suggestions, such as 'Sudan' or 'Nubia', have been made in recent years, and have found their ways into a number of modern translations. A more radical suggestion has quite recently come from a Nigerian Old Testament scholar, Professor David T. Adamo, who argues that Old Testament Cush should be rendered 'Africa'. Adamo's suggestion has, as far as I know, not yet found its way into any translation of the Old Testament, and I will therefore, in the following, give it some comments.

Cush—in history and in the Old Testament

First, some few words about historical Cush and the Old Testament portrayal of Cush.

The African nation Cush, which appears in Assyrian, Egyptian, and Greek sources, as well as in the Old Testament, has a history which can be roughly divided into three periods.[2] In the first period, throughout the

2   For a survey of the history of Cush, see D.B. Redford, "Kush", *The Anchor Bible Dictionary* 4 (1992) 109–111. For further reading, see W.Y. Adams, *Nubia* (1977), and B.G. Trigger, *Nubia under the Pharaohs* (1976).

2nd millennium B.C., Egypt eventually managed to establish some sort of a military control over the areas south of the first and second cataracts on the Nile river, referred to as Cush. Agriculture and trade were encouraged, and large amounts of gold, grain, cattle, incence, ebony, ivory, and slaves from Cush seem to have played a major role in the Egyptian economy. To govern these areas, an administration modelled on that of Egypt was developed, headed by the office of a viceroy.

The second period, approximately from the 10th to the 6th centuries B.C., is characterised by civil war and decline in Egypt. This enabled Cush first to gain independence, and then eventually, in the 7th century B.C., to conquer most of Egypt and develop into a great power stretching from central east Africa to the Red Sea in the east and to the Mediterranean in the north.

The third period in the history of Cush is then a history of decline and withdrawal; from the mid-7th century B.C., when the Assyrians drove the Cushites back into central east Africa, to the 4th century A.D., when Cush finally was defeated by the kingdom of Axum.

From our perspective, as translators and interpreters of the Old Testament, it should be noted that Cush experienced its political greatness in a period close to the period when most of the Old Testament literature originated. It is therefore to be expected that the literary portrayal of Cush in the Old Testament somehow reflects this political greatness. And a brief survey of the Old Testament portrayal of Cush certainly confirms this.

- *Geographically*, Cush is thought of as far away. It is the huge land south of Egypt (Ezekiel 29:10), representing the very south in the Old Testament map of the world (Isaiah 11:11, Zephaniah 2:4–15.12), even being the border of the mighty Persian empire, which stretched from India to Cush (Esther 1:1).
- *Anthropologically*, Cush is connected with black and tall peoples. The Cushites can be depicted as "tall and smooth-skinned" (Isaiah 18:2), and a proverb asks rhetorically: "Can the Cushite change his skin or the leopard its spots?" (Jeremiah 13:23).
- *Politically*, Cush is known for its military abilities, and thereby its potential as a coalition partner. Judah is warned against trusting in Cush instead of Yahweh (Isaiah 20), but Cush can also be of assistance to Judah (2 Kings 19:9 ff.; 2 Samuel 18:21–32).
- *Economically*, Cush is connected with wealth; the merchandise of Cush is well-known (Isaiah 43:3, 45:14, Daniel 11:43).

From Cush to 'Ethiopia', 'Sudan', 'Nubia', and 'Africa'

The Old Testament conception of Cush as a great and mighty nation south of Egypt, inhabited by black peoples, corresponds to some extent to the views of travellers from other countries. The Greeks referred to these black peoples from east and central Africa as *aithiops* (compare Ethiopia)—which probably means "those with burnt faces", whereas the Arabs, a millennium later, talked about *bilad al-sudan* (compare Sudan)—that is, "the land of the black men".

The Graeco-Roman world was well acquainted with the existence of black peoples from east and central Africa, and Graeco-Roman sources often refer to Ethiopia and Ethiopians.[3] Examples from the 6th and 5th centuries B.C. are Xenophanes and Herodotus. Herodotus travelled widely in North Africa; in Egypt he went as far as Aswan (cf. his Books II and III). His writings contain interesting observations concerning the history, culture, and religion of the Ethiopians, as well as their physical characteristics. According to Herodotus (II:22), the Ethiopians

[...] are black by reason of the heat

Xenophanes combined observations concerning the religion of the Ethiopians and on their physical characteristics, remarking:

The Ethiopians say that their gods are stub-nosed and black, the Tracians that theirs have light blue eyes and red hair.[4]

Accordingly, when the Alexandrian translators of the Septuagint in the 3rd and 2nd centuries B.C. had to find Greek counterparts to the Cush of the Hebrew Old Testament, 'Ethiopia' and 'Ethiopian' were natural choices. This rendering has been followed by most translations, from the Vulgate, through, for exampel, the King James version, and up to for example the Contemporary English Bible (US 1995, UK 1996); the latter, however, with a footnote reading:

The Hebrew text has 'Cush', which was a region south of Egypt that included parts of the present countries of Ethiopia and Sudan.

---

3   For a most useful analysis, see F.M. Snowden Jr., *Blacks in antiquity* (1970).

4   Fragment 16, Clement of Alexandria, *Strom*ateis vii:22.1. For an introduction, see G.S. Kirk & J.E. Raven, *The Presocratic Philosophers* (1971) 163–181.

In recent years, some new translations have exchanged 'Ethiopia' for 'Sudan'. Good News Bible / Today's English Version did so in its first edition. However, in the 2nd edition (US 1992, UK 1994) it went back to 'Ethiopia', with a footnote referring to a Word List entry which reads:

> *Ethiopia*: The ancient name of the extensive territory south of the First Cataract of the River Nile was Cush. This region was called Ethiopia in Graeco-Roman times, and included within its borders most of modern Sudan and some of present-day Ethiopia (Abyssinia).

Others, such as the new Norwegian (1978) and Danish (1993) translations, have chosen 'Nubia', whereas the New English Bible varies between 'Nubia' and 'Cush'. This latter option, a transliteration, has also gained some influence, and is chosen by for example the New International Version and the German *Einheitsübersetzung* (1984).

Hesitation between these various options is also reflected in resource material published by the United Bible Societies (UBS). One example could be found in the UBS Handbook on the Book of Amos, where Jan de Waard and William A. Smalley argue that it is "approximately correct" to render the Cush in Amos 9:7 as 'Ethiopia', but that it is also possible, "but not quite as correct", to render it 'Sudan'.[5] Similarily, in the UBS Handbook on the Book of Psalms, Robert G. Bratcher and William D. Reyburn, admit that:

> [...] the territory occupied by the modern country of Sudan more nearly corresponds to the territory south of Egypt occupied by 'Cush'.

Yet, they still argue that the Cush in Psalm 68:31 should be rendered 'Ethiopia'.[6] A third example of this hesitation is found in a 1981 article in *The Bible Translator*, where John A. Thompson argues that 'Sudan' is far better than 'Ethiopia', since Cush according to Ezekiel 29:10:

---

5   J. de Waard & W.A. Smalley, *A translator's handbook on the Book of Amos* (1979) 180.

6   R.G. Bratcher & W.D. Reyburn, *A translator's handbook on the Book of Psalms* (1991) 590–591.

[...] was immediately south of Egypt, that is Nubia or the north Sudan, not the modern Ethiopia which is at least 500 miles from the borders of Egypt in the highlands of east Africa.[7]

A fresh and probably unexpected approach to these questions has then been made by the very productive Nigerian Old Testament scholar, David T. Adamo, currently professor of religious studies at Delta State University in Abraka, Nigeria. In an article published in 1992, Adamo argues that the Hebrew Cush should be rendered 'Africa'.[8] The same idea is also expressed in several of his previous works on what he calls the African presence in the Old Testament.[9]

Adamo first makes a brief survey of the role played by Cush in Egyptian and Assyrian sources and in the Old Testament, where he consistently emphasises aspects favouring an African localisation of Cush.[10] Secondly, he examines Ethiopia in the Graeco-Roman sources, boldly suggesting that the nation called Ethiopia by the ancient writers includes:

[...] all the modern territory [sic!] of the continent of Africa.[11]

Thirdly, having claimed that both 'Cush' in the Ancient Near Eastern sources and 'Ethiopia' in the Graeco-Roman sources to some extent refer to Africa, Adamo concludes that Old Testament Cush should be rendered 'Africa'.[12]

---

7   J.A. Thompson, "Bible geographies and atlases and their use in translating", *The Bible Translator* 32 (1981) 432–433.

8   D.T. Adamo, "Ethiopia in the Bible", *African Christian Studies* 8/II (1992) 51–64.

9   See also D.T. Adamo, *The place of Africa and Africans in the Old Testament and its environment* (1986) *passim*; *idem*, "The African wife of Moses", *Africa Theological Journal* 18 (1989) 230–237; *idem*, "The African queen", *Journal of Arabic and Religious Studies* 7 (1990) 14–24.

10   D.T. Adamo, "Ethiopia in the Bible", *African Christian Studies* 8/II (1992) 51–52.

11   *Ibid.*, 52–57, 57.

12   *Ibid.*, 59–60.

... and back to Cush

Two kinds of problems arise from Adamo's suggestion. First, to render all the Old Testament references to Cush as 'Africa' would create some translation problems. One problem is that it would open up for a never-ending discussion of whether all the Cush-texts in the Old Testament actually refer geographically to Africa. According to Adamo,

> Everywhere the word 'Cush' is used in the Old Testament with a clear cut identification, it refers to Africa.[13]

Nevertheless, one could argue that there remains a number of Cush texts where an African localisation at best is questionable. Another translation problem arises from the fact that the Old Testament uses Cush both as a proper name for individuals and as a name of the people and nation; hence it is difficult to be consequent. Both the Septuagint, the Vulgate, and a number of modern translations distinguish between 'Ethiopia' as the name of the land and nation, for example in Genesis 2:13 or Zephaniah 2:12 and 3:10, and 'Cush' as the name of an individual, for example in Genesis 10:6 or Zephaniah 1:1, whereas all these texts, according to Adamo, should be rendered 'Africa'.[14]

Secondly, to render Cush as 'Africa' would also create some hermeneutical problems. Throughout this century, the very term *Africa* has developed ideologically pregnant connotations, both politically (for example in the term *pan-Africanism*) and theologically (for example in the term *African theology*), and a rendering of Cush as 'Africa' would bring these connotations into the Old Testament texts. On the one hand, texts such as Genesis 2:13, where Cush is related to the Garden of Eden, and Amos 9:7, where Cush and Israel are equated, would probably be experienced positively, and would strengthen the concept of a close relationship between Africa and the Old Testament. On the other hand, texts such as 2 Chronicles 14:8–14, where Cush is depicted as an enemy

---

13   *Ibid.*, 51.

14   D.T. Adamo, *The place of Africa and Africans in the Old Testament and its environment* (1986) 79, 94, and 209; see also his "The black prophet in the Old Testament", *Journal of Arabic and Religious Studies* 4 (1987) 1–8; "Ancient Africa and Genesis 2:10–14", *Journal of Religious Thought* 49 (1992) 33–43; "The Table of nations reconsidered in African perspective", *Journal of African Religion and Philosophy* 2 (1993) 138–143.

of Israel, would create difficulties. The hermeneutical problems already facing contemporary Egyptian and Palestinian readers of the Old Testament when they identify themselves with the ancient Egyptians, Philstines, or Canaanites, that is, enemies of God's chosen people in the Old Testament, would then suddenly be transferred to the whole of Africa.

In the light of these considerations, I would argue that the best solution for the translator is to let Cush remain 'Cush'; that is, to avoid the problems of finding a modern equivalent such as 'Ethiopia', 'Nubia', 'Sudan', or even 'Africa', and just transliterate it. Adamo would certainly oppose this, arguing that the translator should "[...] avoid meaningless words which could not be readily understood by the common readers".[15] Nevertheless, I fear that the costs of rendering Cush with 'Africa' would be greater than the benefits.

Still, Adamo has an important point, and in my opinion his suggestion clearly deserves further attention. On the one hand, I would argue that Old Testament translations should inform their readers, in footnotes or supplements, that Cush in most cases refers to an African nation that is well attested also in extra-biblical sources. On the other hand, I would hope that Old Testament scholars, in Africa as well as in the West, would take up Adamo's suggestion, and further analyse the phenomenon he has pointed out as "the African presence in the Old Testament".

---

[15]   D.T. Adamo, "Ethiopia in the Bible", *African Christian Studies* 8/II (1992) 59.

• 9 •

Is Israel Worth More to God than Cush?
An Interpretation of Amos 9:7

In Amos 9:7 the African people of Cush is related to the people of Israel and to the God of Israel, Yahweh. But what is the meaning of this triangular relationship? A brief glimpse into some of the relevant scholarly literature reveals that this is a relationship with a remarkably divergent history of interpretation. Whereas some interpreters take it as a negative example of Yahweh's judgement over Israel, others take it as a positive example of Yahweh's concern for all peoples, even the remote Cushites. Let me demonstrate this divergent interpretation by quoting two Old Testament scholars; one is a white American writing in 1905, the other is a black African writing in 1998.

The American representative is William R. Harper, a former professor of Semitic languages and literature at the University of Chicago. And, according to Harper, the point of the text is rather negative:

> Israel, says the prophet, is no more to me than the far-distant, uncivilized, and despised black race of the Ethiopians; cf. Je. 13:23. No reference is made to their Hamitic origin or their black skin; and

yet their color and the fact that slaves were so often drawn from them added to the grounds for despising them.[1]

And Harper is not alone. Similar negative interpretations, although not necessarily that vulgar,[2] can be found in devotional as well as critical commentaries throughout the rest of the century.[3]

The African representative is David Tuesday Adamo, professor of Biblical studies at Delta State University, Nigeria. The point of the text, according to Adamo, is much more positive. Yahweh is not

> [...] exclusively bound to one nation, but is master of all and has a special relationship to all. The passage above is one of the occasion[s] where African nations are used 'in terms of their norm for valuation.' The comparison demonstrates that Israel is as precious as Africans before Yahweh.[4]

Neither is Adamo alone. Similar positive interpretations can easily be found within African[5] and African American[6] interpretation, but also

---

1   W.R. Harper, *A critical and exegetical commentary on Amos and Hosea* (1905) 192.

2   Still, Harper is quoted with approval (including his "uncivilized" and "black race") by E. Ullendorff, *Ethiopia and the Bible* (1968) 9, and he is echoed (although without the "uncivilized" and "black race") by J. de Waard & W.A. Smalley, *A translator's handbook on the Book of Amos* (1979) 180: "Israel is put on the same level as the most distant and despised people (the Ethiopians)".

3   Cf. for example J.L. Mays, *Amos: A commentary* (1969) 157; E. Hammershaimb, *The Book of Amos* (1970) 134.

4   D.T. Adamo, *Africa and the Africans in the Old Testament* (1998) 100; cf. also his "Amos 9:7–8 in an African perspective", *Orita* 24 (1992) 76–84.

5   Adamo is indeed the most important exponent of the interest for Cush amongst African exegetes; cf. K. Holter, "Should Old Testament Cush be rendered Africa?", *The Bible Translator* 48 (1997) 331–336; and M. Høyland, "An African presence in the Old Testament?", *Old Testament Essays* 11 (1998) 50–58. However, also other African exegetes have studied the Cush passages, including Amos 9:7a; cf. for example S. Sempore, "Le noir et le salut dans la bible", P. Adeso & al. (eds.), *Universalisme et mission dans la bible* (1993) 17–29.

6   Cf. for example G. Rice, "Was Amos a racist?", *Journal of Religious Thought* 35 (1978) 35–44; R. Smith, "A new perspective on Amos 9:7a", *Journal of the Interdenominational Centre* 22 (1994) 36–47.

within the more traditional guild of western Old Testament interpretation.[7]

The two quotations illustrate the divergent history of interpretation of the triangular relationship between Cush, Israel and Yahweh in Amos 9:7. They also suggest that there is a close connection between the interpreter and his or her interpretation. This should not come as a surprise. With the hermeneutical discussion of the recent decades in mind, one actually expects that a white American, interpreting a text on the African people of Cush a generation after the abolishment of slavery in the USA, would express and emphasise other values and questions than a black African, interpreting the same text a generation after the end of the colonial era of most of Africa. This does not mean that the two interpretations just mirror the contexts of their respective interpreters. It rather reflects the (now obvious) fact that any new interpretative context inevitably lets new values and questions encounter the ancient texts.[8]

In our case this means that we—as interpreters of Amos 9:7 who live in a postcolonial era[9]—should ask ourselves whether the relatively

---

[7]   For research surveys, see Rice and Smith (cf. above, note 6). It should here be noted that Smith, in my view, exaggerates the negative interpretation of Cush in traditional western commentaries on Amos 9:7. One can hardly say, as Smith does, that all those contributions that are listed (pp. 36–37) "[…] have a basic negative connotation." (p. 38). The survey presented by Rice is more balanced. Of western contributions published after Rice's survey, and with a clearly expressed positive understanding of the function of Cush in Amos 9:7, one should note J.A. Soggin, *The Prophet Amos* (1987) 142–144, and especially the thorough discussion in F.I. Anderson & D.N. Freedman, *Amos* (1989) 864–926.

[8]   The African and African American interest for the so-called African (or black) presence in the Old Testament is but one aspect of a more general interest for the portrayal of Africa in ancient texts. One important example here is the Cameroonian theologian E. Mveng, who in the same year as he completed his major study *Les sources grecques de l'histoire négro-africaine depuis Homère jusqu'à Strabon* (1972), also published a paper on "La Bible et l'Afrique noire", cf. E. Mveng & R.J.Z. Werblowsky (eds.), *The Jerusalem Congress* (1972) 23–39. Also the more extreme versions of this interest for Africa in ancient texts, reflected not least in M. Bernal's *Black Athena* (1987 & 1991), have their counterparts in biblical studies; cf. for example W.A. McCray, *The black presence in the Bible* (1990). For critical responses to Bernal, cf. M.R. Lefkowitz & G. MacLean Rogers (eds.), *Black Athena revisited* (1996); and A. Bach, "Whitewashing Athena: Gaining perspective on Bernal and the Bible", *Journal for the Study of the Old Testament* 77 (1998) 3–19.

[9]   The expression "postcolonial era" is here used simply to delimit the decades following the independence of Africa in the 1960s. For a presentation of a more ideologically profiled use of "postcolonialism" with regard to biblical

strong tradition within Old Testament interpretation of seeing slavery or other expressions of humiliation wherever the African nation of Cush occurs, may possibly reflect a western colonial understanding of Africa and Africans.[10] That question is obviously, in its entirety, too large an enterprise for a brief article. Still, one aspect of that large enterprise could be to discuss the initial question: Is Israel worth more to God than Cush? Or, to dress the question in a more exegetical clothing: What is the function of Cush vs Israel and Yahweh in Amos 9:7? In the following pages that question will be discussed—through a close reading of the text, and in the light of some lines in its literary and historical context.

The text

The Cush text (v. 7a) is the first part of a line-pair (v. 7a+b) where both lines somehow relate Israel to one or two foreign nations.

7a *hlwʾ kbny kšyym ʾtm ly bny ysrʾl nʾm yhwh*
7b *hlwʾ ʾt-ysrʾl hʿlyty mʾrṣ mṣrym wplštyym mkptwr wʾrm mqyr*

7a Are you not like the children of the Cushites to me,
    O children of Israel? says Yahweh.
7b Did I not bring Israel up from the land of Egypt,
    and the Philistines from Caphtor and the Arameans from Kir?

Israel occurs in both lines, and she is related to the geographically distant Cushites in line a and to the geographically closer Philistines and Arameans in line b. However, besides the obvious geographical orientation (Cushites—south, Philistines—west, Arameans—north), the

---

interpretation, cf. K. Holter, "Some recent studies on postcolonialism and biblical scholarship", *Newsletter on African Old Testament Scholarship* 5 (1998) 20–23, where I discuss two recent essay collections, L.E. Donaldson (ed.), *Postcolonialism and scriptural reading* (1996) and R.S. Sugirtharajah (ed.), *The Postcolonial Bible* (1998).

10 Older commentaries are full of examples of this phenomenon; one illustrative case could be what the commentaries say about the Cushite officer of David in 2 Samuel 18: H.P. Smith, writing a century ago, is quite certain about the status of this officer: "Joab then calls a negro (naturally a slave)", cf. his *A critical and exegetical commentary on the Books of Samuel* (1898) 359. G.B. Caird, writing half a century later, is not that certain: "The Cushite was an Ethiopian, probably a slave", cf. his "The First and Second Books of Samuel" (1953) 1142.

actual function of the relationship between Israel and these nations, and
also the relationship between the Cushites of line a and the Philistines
and Arameans of line b, is not easy to grasp, as the structure of the text
reflects a rather sophisticated composition. It should, however, be
emphasised that the Masoretic text is clearly understandable, so there is
no need for emendations.[11]

First, one notices that there are several examples of parallels. The
most obvious one is the interrogative *hlwʾ* (the interrogative particle *h* +
the negation *lwʾ*; "are you not?" ‖ "did I not?") that opens both lines.[12]
The function of these introductory interrogatives is that they bind the two
lines to each other and thereby indicate some kind of parallelism.[13]
Another example, strengthening the paralleling function of these
introductory interrogatives, is that both lines let Yahweh be the speaking
subject,[14] to which first Israel and Cush (line a: *ly*, "to me") and then
Israel and the Philistines/Arameans (line b: *hʿlyty*, "I [...] bring") are
related. A third example is that each line has its own set of parallels; both
are linked to a comparison between Israel and the nations. First, line a
lets the double construct chain *bny* + nation ("children of Cush" ‖

---

11   I emphasise this against attempts from older interpreters to emend the Hebrew text
     of v. 7a; their emendations are generally built on a negative understanding of Cush,
     rather than a need to make sense out of a corrupt text. Cf. for example A.B. Ehrlich,
     Randglossen zur Hebräischen Bibel ([1912] 1968) 254, who renders v. 7a as
     "betragt ihr euch nicht gegen mich wie die Kuschiter, ihr Kinder Israel?"; and also
     V. Maag, *Text, Wortschatz und Begriffswelt des Buches Amos* (1951) 58–59 (cf.
     also p. 160), who renders v. 7a as "Soviel wie Neger geltet ihr mir, ihr Israeliten".

12   According to *Gesenius-Kautzsch* § 150e, the function of these interrogatives is to
     express the conviction that the content of the statement is unconditionally admitted
     by the hearer. This has lead R. Smith, "A new perspective on Amos 9:7a", *Journal
     of the Interdenominational Centre* 22 (1994) 46, to argue that the introductory *hlwʾ*
     ought to be given an affirmative rather than interrogative translation: "You are just
     like the Kushites to me." In my opinion it is unnecessary to bring this interpretation
     into the translation; it has, for example, no support in the ancient *versiones*. Still,
     whatever translation is chosen, the double introductory *hlwʾ* serves to parallel the
     two lines.

13   A corresponding example is found in Amos 3:3–5, where a series of no less than 5x
     introductory interrogatives serves to bind together and parallel the five lines. This
     function of the 5x introductory interrogatives is then strengthened by other syntactic
     parallels, especially by the 5x *yqtl* verbs and the 5x negations.

14   Line a refers to Yahweh in third person ("says the Lord"), and line b in first person
     ("did I not").

"children of Israel") compare Israel and Cush; the explicit sign of the comparison is here the comparative particle *k* [+ *bny kšyym*]. And then, line b lets the triple prepositional *m*[*n*] + nation ("from Egypt" ‖ "from Caphtor" ‖ "from Kir") compare Israel and the Philistines/Arameans; the explicit sign of the comparison is here the double copulative *w* [+ *plštyym* ... + *ʾrm*]. Taken together, these two sets of parallels serve to strengthen the paralleling of lines a and b.

Secondly, however, one also notices that there are some examples of structures that break the direct parallelism between the two lines. One is that line a is a nominal clause, whereas line b is a verbal clause. Another is that the text is constructed as a chiasm around "Israel"; line a has "nation + Israel", whereas line b turns this to "Israel + 3x nations". I would, however, be somewhat hesitant about concluding that these structural features express a contrast between the two lines, that is, a contrast between line a's relation of Israel to Cush and line b's relation of Israel to the Philistines and Arameans. With regard to the nominal vs verbal clauses, one could possibly argue that the nominal line a expresses a general state or condition, whereas the verbal line b points back to more specific experiences of the past. However, with regard to the chiasm, there are no textual signs that demand a contrasting interpretation.

Summing up, a reading of line a gives us a comparison between Israel and Cush—a comparison linked to their mutual relationship with Yahweh. Line b then presents Israel's major salvation experience as but one of several examples of Yahweh's concern for a particular people. Reading both lines together, the parallelism between the two links the comparison between Cush and Israel—and their mutual relationship with Yahweh (line a), to a context that expresses a positive concern of Yahweh for Israel as well as for other peoples (line b). It should here be emphasised that there is nothing in the text which questions Yahweh's relationship with Israel. However, at the same time the text presents the relationship between Yahweh and other nations in expressions that parallel Israel and these nations. Accordingly, the election of Israel does not exclude Yahweh from having a similar relationship with other nations.

The text and its literary context

In an attempt to organise the literary context of the Cush-text in Amos 9:7, it will be read in the light of two concentric circles; first its

immediate context—the book of Amos, and then its broader context—
the Old Testament as a whole.

Within the book of Amos, the only reference to Cush is the one in
9:7. This verse opens what can be said to be the epilogue of the book,
9:7–15. And when v. 7 focuses on the relationship between Israel and
one or more foreign nations, it introduces a central topic of this epilogue.
The concluding verses of the book actually outline Israel's entire Old
Testament history—from the exodus experience (v. 7), through the
monarchy (v. 8: *mmlkh*, cf. 7:13) and the exile (vv. 9–10), and to the
hopes for a post-exilic future (vv. 11–15). And throughout this historical
outline Israel is presented in relation to other nations. In addition to the
southern, western and northern orientation in v. 7, there is also an eastern
orientation in v. 12, as Israel is related to her ancient eastern neighbour,
Edom. And, in between the specified nations of vv. 7 and 12, v. 9 more
generally says that Yahweh will shake Israel "among the nations".

Whereas Cush is not mentioned elsewhere in the book of Amos, the
opposite is the case with the other nations. The references to Israel, the
Philistines and the Arameans in v. 7 echo chiastically the judgement
oracles in chs. 1 and 2: the Arameans (1:3–5), the Philistines (1:6–8), and
Judah/Israel (2:4–5/6–16). Also the reference to Edom in v. 12 has its
counterpart within the judgement oracles, cf. 1:11–12. The function of
these references certainly differ, from the negative—vs all nations in chs
1–2, to the positive—vs some of the same nations in 9:7 and (at least for
Israel, hardly for Edom) in 9:12. Still, the common theological
denominator through all these texts is the idea that Yahweh is
responsible for the history of all nations, not only that of Israel, and
further the idea that all nations, not only Israel, are responsible to
Yahweh.[15]

The idea of comparing Israel to foreign nations both opens (cf. 1:3–
2:16) and closes (cf. 9:7) the book of Amos, and in between one finds a
theology where aspects of universalism (cf. especially the doxologies,
4:13, 5:8–9, 9:5–6) and particularism (cf. especially 3:2) exist side by
side. In other words, although Yahweh has a special relationship with
Israel, he has indeed also a relationship with other nations. This provides
a reasonable context for the triangular relationship between Cush, Israel
and Yahweh in 9:7, as Cush then can be understood as an

---

15 H. Gese, "Das problem von Amos 9,7", *Alttestamentliche Studien* (1991) 116–121,
p. 119, has noted that a similar concept is expressed in Deuteronomy 2, where vv. 5,
9, 12 and 19 say that Israel should not take the land of the Edomites, Moabites and
Ammonites, as these nations have been given their land by Yahweh.

exemplification of Yahweh's relationship with other nations. Still, in order to get a broader background for understanding the particular mentioning of Cush, it is necessary to proceed to the next circle around 9:7, the Old Testament as a whole, and its more frequently occurring references to Cush.

The Old Testament has 56 references to Cush/Cushi,[16] and, taken together, these references are able to give a many-faceted portrayal. Geographically, Cush is thought of as far away; it is the huge land south of Egypt (cf. Ezekiel 29:10), representing the very south of the Old Testament map of the world (cf. Isaiah 11:11, Zephaniah 2:4–15, 12). It is even used to demarcate the borders of the mighty Persian empire, which is said to stretch from India to Cush (cf. Esther 1:1, 8:9). Anthropologically, Cush is connected with black peoples; it is "a people tall and smooth-skinned" (Isaiah 18:2). Politically, Cush is associated with its military abilities. Its potential as a coalition partner is of importance; negatively Judah is warned against trusting in Cush instead of Yahweh (cf. Isaiah 20), but positively Cush can also be of assistance to Judah (cf. 2 Kings 19:9 ff. and 2 Samuel 18:21–32). Finally, economically, Cush is connected with wealth; the merchandise of Cush is referred to as a well-known entity (cf. Isaiah 45:14, 43:3, and Daniel 11:43).

Now, is it possible—within this Old Testament portrayal of Cush—to find texts that can throw light on the triangular relationship of Cush to Israel and Yahweh in Amos 9:7? First, the idea of a comparison between Cush and Israel is reflected in at least two other texts. One is Jeremiah 13:23, quoting a proverb that asks rhetorically "Can a Cushite change his skin or the leopard its spots?", and where the supposed negative response is used to point out that Jerusalem can no more change her evil ways than the Cushite can change the colour of his skin. Although the context here is negative, the actual comparison of Jerusalem to a Cushite has no negative connotations. Another text is Isaiah 43:3, where Cush together with two other African nations, Egypt and Seba, is depicted as the ransom Yahweh is willing to give to the Persian king Cyrus to gain the release of exiled Israel. And here Cush most definitively plays a positive

---

[16] Cush: Genesis 2:13, 10:6.7.8, 2 Kings 19:9, Isaiah 11:11, 18:1, 20:3.4.5, 37:9, 43:3, 45:14, Jeremiah 36:14, 46:9, Ezekiel 29:10, 30:4.5.9, 38:5, Nahum 3:9, Zephaniah 3:10, Psalms 7:1, 68:32, 87:4, Job 28:19, Esther 1:1, 8:9, 1 Chronicles 1:8.9.10. Cushi: Numbers 12:1.1, 2 Samuel 18:21.21.22.23.31.32.32, Jeremiah 13:23, 38:7.10.12, 39:16, Amos 9:7, Zephaniah 1:1, 2:12, Daniel 11:43, 2 Chronicles 12:3, 14:8.11.12.12, 16:8, 21:16.

role. When v. 3 uses the word "ransom" (*kpr*), it continues the idea of Yahweh as "redeeming" (*g²l*) Israel in v. 1, and it leads up to v. 4, where Yahweh says that he will give "peoples" (*l²mym*) instead of Israel. This redemption of Israel reflects Yahweh's love—"you are precious and honoured in my sight" (v. 4), and the valuable compensation that had to be paid for Israel is Cush and the two other African nations. Accordingly, the comparison between Israel and Cush in Amos 9:7 is not the only example; there are some few others elsewhere in the Old Testament, and then with more or less positive connotations.

Secondly, the idea of Cush having a relationship to Yahweh is reflected several times in the Old Testament. A negative example is the narrative in 2 Chronicles 14:9–15, where Zerah the Cushite marches out against king Asa of Judah, and where Yahweh finally "struck down the Cushites before Asa and Judah" (v. 12). However, other texts are much more positive. The Old Testament concept of a pilgrimage of the nations to Zion also includes Cush. One example is found in Isaiah 18, where a vivid description of the Cushites as "an aggressive nation of strange speech" concludes that even this nation will bring gifts to Yahweh at Mount Zion. Other examples are found in the Psalms; in Psalm 87 Cush is one of the nations about which it is said: "This one is born in Zion" (v. 4), and in Psalm 68 it is said that "Cush will submit herself to God" (v. 32, ET 31). Accordingly, the portrayal of Cush vs Yahweh in Amos 9:7 reflects a rather general concept of the Old Testament: Foreign nations do indeed have a relationship with Yahweh. Sometimes they may be portrayed as enemies of Yahweh (and Israel) or as instruments in Yahweh's hands (vs Israel); still, other times they may be portrayed as participants in the eschatological pilgrimage to Zion, receiving the blessings of Yahweh.

Summing up, a reading of Amos 9:7 in the light of its immediate (Amos) as well as broader (Old Testament) literary contexts, suggests that its triangular relationship between Cush, Israel and Yahweh can be taken as a positive example of a more general universalism.

The text and its historical context

Most of the Old Testament references to Cush and Cushites refer to an African[17] nation well known from Egyptian, Assyrian and Greek

---

17   Also other possibilities than an African location have been discussed with regard to Old Testament Cush, for example the Kassites in Babylon or a tribal group

sources.[18] This nation was situated south of Egypt; its heartland was the area between the first and sixth cataracts of the Nile. Throughout the third and second millennia B.C. there were close connections between these areas and the mighty neighbour in the north. Historians have traditionally seen these connections from the perspective of a superior Egyptian culture and political system. In recent years, however, some scholars have argued that Cush and Egypt instead should be seen as more equal rivals, competing for some of the same resources and lands along the Nile.[19]

The history of Cush can roughly be divided in three. (1) From the third millennium B.C. to the 10th century B.C. Cush can be described as being at the edge of the Egyptian civilisation; from the 16th century it was a province under Egypt, and Egyptian texts show that Cush in this period supplied Egypt with different kinds of food, in addition to gold and ivory. (2) The civil war and general decline in Egypt from the 10th century B.C. enabled Cush to develop into an independent nation, and then eventually in the 7th century B.C. to conquer most of Egypt and for a short while establish a great power stretching from central east Africa to the Red Sea in the east and to the Mediterranean in the north; the 25th, Cushite dynasty. (3) And then, finally, from the 650s to the 320s B.C., Cush experienced a decay. It was thrown out of Egypt by Assyria, and it was finally conquered by the kingdom of Axum (ca. 350 A.D.).

What, then, does this historical context mean for the reader searching for the function of Cush in Amos 9:7? That, of course, depends on where we place the reader![20] A reader (or listener!) in the mid-eighth

supposed to have lived on the south-western border of Judah, and in some cases a non-African location seems reasonable. For a survey, cf. J. Simons, *The geographical and topographical texts of the Old Testament* (1959) 18–21; for further discussion, cf. S. Hidal, "The land of Cush in the Old Testament", *Svensk Exegetisk Årsbok* 41–42 (1977) 97–106.

[18] For introductory surveys, cf. for example D.B. Redford, "Kush", *The Anchor Bible Dictionary* 4 (1992) 109–111; and J.D. Hays, "The Cushites", *Bibliotheca Sacra* 153 (1996) 270–280. A comprehensive study of the textual and archaeological sources has recently been presented by L. Török, *The Kingdom of Kush* (1997).

[19] Cf. D. O'Connor, *Ancient Nubia* (1993).

[20] For surveys of the contact between Cush and Israel, cf. R.A. "Bennett, Africa and the Biblical period", *Harvard Theological review* 64 (1971) 483–500; C.B. Copher, "The Bible and the African experience", *Journal of the Interdenominational Theological Centre* 16 (1988/1989) 32–50; R.W. Anderson, "Zephaniah ben Cushi and Cush of Benjamin", S.W. Holloway & L.K. Handy (eds.), *The pitcher is broken* (1995) 45–70.

century, contemporary with the prophet, would probably be a bit too early to know the Cushite dynasty that took over Egypt. The hegemony of Kashta the Cushite (mid-eighth century) was acknowledged at Elephantine, but it was during the reigns of Piankhy (735–712 B.C.) and Shabako (712–698 B.C.) that the invasion of Egypt was completed. Still, the growing independence and military as well as economic strength of the Cushites may have been known already to the first readers of the text. A later reader, for example in the mid-sixth century B.C., would be familiar with some of the traditions about the victorious Cushites; the nation in the far south had been able to conquer its former conquerors, the mighty Egyptians. A comparison with this nation would obviously be of inspiration to a people in captivity, hoping for a new exodus!

Conclusion

Now, is Israel—actually—worth more to God than other nations, for example the African nation of Cush? There is, of course, no easy answer to that question. Still, it seems clear that the function of Cush vs Israel and Yahweh in Amos 9:7 is to present a positive parallel to Israel; such an interpretation of the triangular relationship fits the universalistic tendencies in the Book of Amos, it has textual counter-parts elsewhere in the Old Testament, and it gives meaning in different historical contexts.

In recent years the so-called African presence in the Old Testament has received some attention from African and African American scholars. A text like Amos 9:7 is then important, as it reflects the challenge to further study from exegetical as well as hermeneutical perspectives.

Bibliography

Abe, G.O., *Covenant in the Old Testament*. Unpubl. diss. University of Ibadan, 1983.

———, "Berith: Its impact on Israel and its relevance to the Nigerian society", *African Journal of Biblical Studies* 1/I (1986) 66–73.

———, "Religion and national unity: Guidelines for Nigeria from the Judean exilic and post-exilic experience", *Africa Theological Journal* 15 (1986) 63–72.

———, "The Jewish and Yoruba social institution of marriage: A comparative study", *Orita* 21 (1989) 3–18.

———, "African Journal of Biblical Studies", *Newsletter on African Old Testament Scholarship* 3 (1997) 12–13.

Abegunde, S.O., *A philosophy and method of translating the Old Testament into Yoruba*. Unpubl. diss. Southern Baptist Theological Seminary, 1985.

Abogunrin, S.O., "Biblical research in Africa: The task ahead", *African Journal of Biblical Studies* 1/I (1986) 7–24.

Abotchie, F.F.K., "Rites of passage and socio-cultural organization in African culture and Judaism", F. von Hammerstein (ed.), *Christian-*

Jewish relations in ecumenical perspective, with special emphasis on Africa. Geneva: World Council of Churches (1978) 82–89.

Adamo, D.T., "The black prophet in the Old Testament", *Journal of Arabic and Religious Studies* 4 (1987) 1–8.

———, "The African wife of Moses: An examination of Numbers 12:1–9", *Africa Theological Journal* 18 (1989) 230–237.

———, "Understanding the Genesis creation account in an African background", *Carribean Journal of Religious Studies* 10 (1989) 17–25.

———, "The African queen (I Kings 10:10–13, II Chronicles 9:1–12)", *Journal of Arabic and Religious Studies* 7 (1990) 14–24.

———, "Amos 9:7–8 in an African perspective", *Orita* 24 (1992) 76–84.

———, "Ancient Africa and Genesis 2:10–14", *Journal of Religious Thought* 49 (1992) 33–43.

———, "Ethiopia in the Bible", *African Christian Studies* 8/II (1992) 51–64.

———, "The distinctive use of Psalms in Africa", *Melanesian Journal of Theology* 9 (1993) 94–11.

———, "The table of nations reconsidered in African perspective (Genesis 10)", *Journal of African Religion and Philosophy* 2 (1993) 138–143.

———, "Doing Old Testament research in Africa", *Newsletter on African Old Testament Scholarship* 3 (1997) 8–11.

———, *Africa and the Africans in the Old Testament*. San Francisco: Christian Universities Press, 1998 [revised version of his *The place of Africa and Africans in the Old Testament and its environment*. Ph.D. diss., Baylor University, Waco, 1986].

Adams, W., *Nubia: Corridor to Africa*. London: Allen Lane, 1977.

de Adegbola, E.A.A. (ed.), *Traditional religion in West Africa*. Ibadan: Daystar Press, 1983.

Adelowo, E.D., "A comparative study of creation stories in Yoruba religion, Islam and Judaeo-Christianity", *Africa Theological Journal* 15 (1986) 29–53.

———, "Death and burial in Yoruba, Quranic and biblical religion", *Orita* 19 (1987) 104–117.

Ademiluka, S., "The use of therapeutic psalms in inculturating Christianity in Africa", *African Ecclesiastical Review* 37 (1995) 221–227.

Adutwum, O., *The root* בטח *in the Old Testament*. Unpubl. diss. University of Hamburg, 1984.

———, "The suspected adulteress: Ancient Israelite and traditional Akan treatment", *The Expository Times* 104 (1992/1993) 38–42.

Ajayi, J.F. Ade & al., *The African experience with higher education*. Accra: The Association of African Universities, 1996.

Akao, J.O., "The letter of Aristeas and its worth in biblical studies", *Orita* 22/I (1990) 52–63.

Akpunonu, P.D., *Salvation in Deutero-Isaiah*. Unpubl. diss. Pontificia Universitas Urbaniana, Rome, 1971.

Alao, D., "The relevance of the Amarna letters to Hebrew origins", *Orita* 16/II (1984) 87–97.

Anderson, F.I. & Freedman, D.N., *Amos: A new translation with introduction and commentary*. New York etc.: Doubleday, 1989 (The Anchor Bible; 24A).

Anderson, R.W., "Zephaniah ben Cushi and Cush of Benjamin: Traces of a Cushite presence in Syria-Palestine", S.W. Holloway & L.K. Handy (eds.), *The pitcher is broken: Memorial essays for Gösta W. Ahlström*. Sheffield: Sheffield Academic Press (1995) 45–70 (Journal for the Study of the Old Testament. Supplement Series; 190).

Assimeng, M., *Saints and social structures*. Legon: Ghana Publishing Corporation, 1986.

Atal Sa Angang, D. (ed.), *Christianisme et identité africaine. Point de vue exegetique. Actes du 1er congres des biblistes africains*. Kinshasa: Faculte de theologie catholique, 1980.

Atteh, S.O., "The crisis in higher education in Africa", *Issue: Quarterly Journal of Opinion* 24 (1996) 36–42.

Bach, A., "Whitewashing Athena: Gaining perspective on Bernal and the Bible", *Journal for the Study of the Old Testament* 77 (1998) 3–19.

Bailey, R.C., "Beyond identification: The use of Africans in Old Testament poetry and narratives", C.H. Felder (ed.), *Stony the road we trod: African American biblical interpretation*. Minneapolis: Fortress Press (1991) 165–184.

Bajeux, J.-C., "Mentalité noire et mentalité biblique", A. Abble & al. (eds.), *Des prêtres noirs s'interrogent*. Paris: Les éditions de cerf (1956) 57–82.

Barret, D.B., *Schism and renewal in Africa: An analysis of six thousand contemporary religious movements*. Nairobi: Oxford University Press, 1968.

Bates, M.S., *Survey of the training of the ministry in Africa. Part II*. London & New York: International Missionary Council, 1954.

Bediaku, B.J.B., *Etude comparé de la célébration pénitentielle dans l'ancient testament et chez le peuple Ewe du Togo. Pour une cathéchèse de la célébration pénitentielle en afrique noire*. Unpubl. diss. Academia Alfonsiana, Rome, 1978.

Bennett, R.A., "Africa and the Biblical period", *Harvard Theological Review* 64 (1971) 483–500.

Bernal, M., *Black Athena: The Afroasiatic roots of classical civilization*. New Brunswick: Rutgers University Press, 1987 [vol. 1] & 1991 [vol. 2].

Blum, W.G., *Forms of marriage: Monogamy reconsidered*. Eldoret: AMECEA Gaba Publications, 1989 (Spearhead Series; 105–107).

Boulaga, F.E., *Christianity without fetishes: An African critique and recapture of Christianity*. Maryknoll: Orbis Books, 1984.

Bowen, D.N., "Old Testament literature in the NEGST library", *Newsletter on African Old Testament Scholarship* 4 (1998) 20–21.

Bowers, P., "New light on theological education in Africa", *Evangelical Review of Theology* 14 (1990) 57–63.

Bratcher, R.G. & Reyburn, W.D., *A translator's handbook on the Book of Psalms*. New York: United Bible Societies, 1991.

Burden, J.J., "Are Shem and Ham blood brothers? The relevance of the Old Testament to Africa", *Old Testament Essays* 1 (1983) 49–72.

———, "World-view in interpreting the Old Testament in Africa", *Old Testament Essays* 4 (1986) 95–110.

Bürkle, H., "Patterns of sermons from various parts of Africa", D.B. Barret (ed.), *African initiatives in religion*. Nairobi (1971) 222–231.

Caird, G.B., "The First and Second Books of Samuel", *The Interpreter's Bible*, vol. 2, New York: Abingdon Press, 1953.

Carter, C.E. & Meyers, C.L. (eds.), *Community, identity, and ideology: Social science approaches to the Hebrew Bible*. Wiona Lake: Eisenbrauns, 1996 (Sources for Biblical and Theological Studies; 6).

Clignet, R., "On dit que la polygamie est morte: Vive la polygamie!", D. Parkin & D. Nyamwaya (eds.), *Transformations of African marriage*. Manchester: Manchester University Press (1987) 199–209 (International African Seminars New Series; 3).

Cogan, M., "The other Egypt: A welcome asylum", M.V. Fox & al. (eds.), *Texts, temples, and tradition: A tribute to Menahem Haran*. Wiona Lake: Eisenbrauns (1996) 65–70.

Copher, C.B., "The Bible and the African experience", *Journal of the Interdenominational Theological Centre* 16 (1988/1989) 32–50.

———, *Black biblical studies: An anthology*. Chicago: Black Light Fellowship, 1993.

Conradie, E.M., "Tracy's notion of dialogue: 'Our last, best hope'?", *Scriptura* 57 (1996) 149–178.

Currid, J.D., *Ancient Egypt and the Old Testament*. Grand Rapids: Baker Books, 1997.

Deist, F.E., "South African Old Testament studies and the future", *Old Testament Essays* 5 (1992) 311–331.

———, *Ervaring, rede en metode in Skrifuitleg: 'N wetenskapshistoriese ondersoek na Skrifuitleg in die Ned Geref Kerk 1840–1990*. Pretotia: RGN, 1994.

———, "Biblical interpretation in post-colonial Africa", *Svensk Teologisk Kvartalskrift* 72 (1996) 110–118.

Dickson, K.A., "African traditional religions and the Bible", E. Mveng & R.Z. Werblowsky (eds.), *The Jerusalem congress on Black Africa and the Bible*. Jerusalem: Anti-Defamation League of B'nai B'rit (1972) 155–166.

———, "The Old Testament and African Theology", *Ghana Bulletin of Theology* 4 (1973) 31–41.

———, "'Hebrewisms of West Africa': The Old Testament and African life and thought", *Legon Journal of Humanities* 1 (1974) 23–34.

————, "Continuity and discontinuity between the Old Testament and African life and thought", *Bulletin of African Theology* 1 (1979) 179–193.

————, *Theology in Africa*. Maryknoll: Orbis Books, 1984.

Djitangar, E.E., "La mission de serviteur de Yahweh: Is. 42:1–9", P. Adeso & al. (eds.), *Universalisme et mission dans la bible*. Nairobi: Catholic Biblical Centre for Africa and Madagascar (1993) 30–39.

Domatob, J.K., "Policy issues for African universities", *Issue: Quarterly Journal of Opinion* 24 (1996) 29–35.

Donaldson, L.E. (ed.), *Postcolonialism and scriptural reading*. Atlanta: Society of Biblical Literature, 1996 [= *Semeia* 75].

Draper, J.A., "Confessional Western text-centered biblical interpretation and oral or residual-oral context", *Semeia* 73 (1996) 59–77.

Dubois, M.J., "La Bible comme evenement transcendent et la culture", E. Mveng & R.J.Z. Werblowsky, *The Jerusalem congress on Black Africa and the Bible*. Jerusalem: Anti-Defamation League of B'nai B'rit (1972) 47–59.

Ebo, D.J.I., *'O that Jacob would survive': A study on hope in the Book of Amos*. Unpubl. diss. University of Nigeria, 1985.

————, "Another look at Amos' visions", *Africa Theological Journal* 18/I (1989) 17–27.

Ehret, C., "Ancient Egyptian as an African language, Egypt as an African culture", T. Celenko (ed.), *Egypt in Africa*. Indianapolis: Indiana University Press (1996) 25–27.

Ehrlich, A.B., *Randglossen zur Hebräischen Bibel*. Vol. 5. Hildesheim: Georg Olms Verlagsbuchhandlung 1968 [repr. of 1st. ed., Leipzig, 1912].

Ekpo, M.U., "Robertson Smith, the 'higher critics' and the problem of prophecy: A case study in the sociology of knowledge", *Africa Theological Journal* 14/II (1985) 79–90.

Ela, J.-M., *Le cri de l'homme africain. Paris: Librarie-Editions L'Harmattan 1980*.

Engelken, K., "פִּלֶגֶשׁ", *Theologisches Wörterbuch zum Alten Testament* 6 (1989) 586–589.

Enomate, J.M., "Ezra the scribe: A reconsideration", *African Journal of Biblical Studies* 1/II (1986) 148–159.

Eribo, F., "Higher education in Nigeria: Decades of development and decline", *Issue: Quarterly Journal of Opinion* 24 (1996) 64–67.

Etuk, E.S., "African universities: problems and solutions", *Issue: Quarterly Journal of Opinion* 24 (1996) 43–44.

Evans-Pritchard, E.E., *Kinship and marriage among the Nuer*. Oxford: Clarendon Press, 1951.

——, *Nuer religion*. Oxford: Oxford University Press, [1956] 1970.

Fasholé-Luke, E.E., "Bible commentary for Africa project", *Exchange* 10 (1981) 42–45.

Felder, C.H., *Troubling biblical waters: Race, class, and family*. Maryknoll: Orbis Books, 1989.

——, (ed.), *Stony the road we trod: African American biblical interpretation*. Minneapolis: Fortress, 1991.

——, "Afrocentrism, the Bible, and the politics of difference", *Journal of Religious Thought* 50 (1993/1994) 45–56.

Fiedler, K., "Postgraduate theology degrees in Malawi", *Religion in Malawi* 5 (1995) 37–41.

—— & Ross, K.R., "Postgraduate theology degrees at the University of Malawi: Vision and reality", *Ministerial Formation* 72 (1996) 15–19.

Fiensy, D., "Using the Nuer culture of Africa in understanding the Old Testament: An evaluation", *Journal for the Study of the Old Testament* 38 (1987) 73–83.

Flint, P.W., "Old Testament scholarship from an African perspective", J.J. Burden (ed.), *Exodus 1–15: Proceedings of the 29th annual congress of the Old Testament Society of South Africa*. Pretoria: Department of Old Testament, UNISA (1987) 179–214 (Old Testament Society of South Africa; 29).

Forslund, E., *The word of God in Ethiopian tongues: Rhetorical features in the preaching of the Ethiopian Evangelical Church Mekane Yesus*. Uppsala: Swedish Institute of Missionary Research, 1993 (Studia Missionalia Uppsaliensia; 58).

Fortes, M., "Kinship and marriage among the Ashanti", A.R. Radcliffe-Brown & D. Forde (eds.), *African systems of kinship and marriage*. Oxford: Oxford University Press (1950) 252–284.

Gakindi, G., *La benediction aaronique et la b^{e}rakah de l'ancien testament*. Unpubl. diss. Yaoundé Faculty of Protestant Theology, Yaoundé, 1992.

Gese, H., "Das problem von Amos 9,7", A.H.J. Gunneweg & O. Kaiser (eds.), *Textgemäss: Aufsätze und Beiträge zur Hermeneutik des Alten Testaments. Festschrift für Ernst Würthwein zum 70. Geburtstag*. Göttingen: Vandenhoeck & Ruprecht (1979) 33–38; repr. in H. Gese, *Alttestamentliche Studien*. Tübingen: J.C.B. Mohr (1991) 116–121.

Gitau, S., *African and biblical understanding of the environment*. Unpubl. diss. University of Nairobi, 1996.

―――― & al., "Contextualized Old Testament programmes?", *Newsletter on African Old Testament Scholarship* 2 (1997) 3–7.

Goba, B., "Corporate personality: Ancient Israel and Africa", B. More (ed.), *Black Theology: The South African voice*. London: C. Hurst & Company (1973) 65–73.

Golka, F.W., *The leopard's spots: Biblical and African wisdom in Proverbs*. Edinburgh: T. & T. Clark, 1993.

Görg, M., "Ofir und Punt", *Biblische Notizen* 82 (1996) 5–8.

Gowan, D.E., *From Eden to Babel: Genesis 1–11*. Grand Rapids: W.B. Eerdmans, 1988 (International Theological Commentary).

Haak, R.H., "'Cush' in Zephaniah", S.W. Holladay & L.K. Handy (eds.), *The pitcher is broken: Memorial essays for Gösta W. Ahlström*. Sheffield: Sheffield Academic Press (1995) 238–251 (Journal for the Study of the Old Testament Supplement Series; 190).

Habtu, T., *A taxonomy of approaches of five representative scholars to the nature of wisdom in the Old Testament, in the light of Proverbs 1–9*. Unpubl. diss. Trinity Evangelical Divinity School, Deerfield, 1993.

Hamilton, V.P., "Marriage: Old Testament and Ancient Near East", *The Anchor Bible Dictionary* 4 (1992) 559–569.

Hammershaimb, E., *The Book of Amos: A commentary*. Oxford: Blackwell, 1970.

von Hammerstein, F. (ed.), *Christian-Jewish relations in ecumenical perspective, with special emphasis on Africa.* Geneva: World Council of Churches, 1978.

Harper, W.R., *A critical and exegetical commentary on Amos and Hosea.* Edinburgh: T. & T. Clark, 1905 (The International Critical Commentary).

Hays, J.D., "The Cushites: A black nation in history", *Bibliotheca Sacra* 153 (1996) 270–280.

———, "The Cushites: A black nation in the Bible", *Bibliotheca Sacra* 153 (1996) 396–409.

Hidal, S., "The land of Cush in the Old Testament", *Svensk Exegetisk Årsbok* 41–42 (1977) 97–106.

Hillman, E., *Polygamy reconsidered: African plural marriage and the Christian churces.* Maryknoll: Orbis Books, 1975.

Hinga, T.M., "'Reading with': An exploration of the interface between 'critical' and 'ordinary' readings of the Bible: A response", *Semeia* 73 (1996) 277–284.

Holter, K., *Tropical Africa and the Old Testament: A select and annotated bibliography.* Oslo: University of Oslo, 1996 (Faculty of Theology: Bibliography Series; 6).

———, (ed.), *Newsletter on African Old Testament Scholarship.* Stavanger, 1996—

———, "Gammeltestamentlig forskning mellom Sahara og Zambezi", *Tidsskrift for teologi og kirke* 68 (1997) 135–146.

———, "Should Old Testament Cush be rendered 'Africa'?", *The Bible Translator* 48 (1997) 331–336.

———, "Afrikansk gammeltestamentlig forskning i spenning mellom Sørs myter og Nords metoder", *Norsk tidsskrift for misjon* 52 (1998) 147–159.

———, "It's not only a question of money! African Old Testament scholarship between the myths and meanings of the South and the money and methods of the North", *Old Testament Essays* 11 (1998) 240–254.

———, "Some recent studies on postcolonialism and biblical scholarship", *Newsletter on African Old Testament Scholarship* 5 (1998) 20–23.

——, "The institutional context of Old Testament scholarship in Africa", *Old Testament Essays* 11 (1998) 452–461.

——, "Africa in the Old Testament", forthcoming in G.O. West & M.W. Dube (eds.), *The Bible in Africa*. Leiden: Brill, 2000.

——, "Old Testament scholarship in Sub-Saharan Africa", forthcoming in G.O. West & M.W. Dube (eds.), *The Bible in Africa*. Leiden: Brill, 2000.

Høyland, M., "An African presence in the Old Testament? David Tuesday Adamo's interpretation of the Old Testament Cush passages", *Old Testament Essays* 11 (1998) 50–58.

Idowu, E.B., "The teaching of the Bible to African students", E. Mveng & R.Z. Werblowsky (eds.), *The Jerusalem congress on Black Africa and the Bible*. Jerusalem: Anti-Defamation League of B'nai B'rit (1972) 199–204.

Ifesieh, E.I., "Web of matrimony in the Bible, social anthropology and African traditional religion", *Communio Viatorum* 26 (1983) 195–211.

Ita, M., "Biblical prophecy and its challenge to contemporary prophetic movements: A lay viewpoint", *Africa Theological Journal* 18 (1989) 3–16.

Jackson, A.A. *Examining the record: An exegetical and homiletical study of blacks in the Bible*. New York: Peter Lang, 1994 (Martin Luther King Jr. Memorial Studies in Religion, Culture and Social Development; 4).

Jonker, L.C., "Bridging the gap between Bible readers and 'professional' exegetes", *Old Testament Essays* 10 (1997) 69–83.

Kalugila, L., *The wise king: Studies in royal wisdom as divine revelation in the Old Testament and its environment*. Lund: CWK Gleerup, 1980 (Coniectanea Biblica Old Testament Series; 15).

Kanyoro, M.R.A., "A proposal for translation research strategy for Africa", *The Bible Translator* 34 (1983) 101–106.

——, "Interpreting Old Testament polygamy through African eyes", M.A. Oduyoye & M.R.A. Kanyoro (eds.), *The will to arise: Women, tradition and the church in Africa*. Maryknoll: Orbis Books (1992) 87–100.

Kawale, W.R., "Divergent interpretations of the relationship between some concepts of God in the Old Testament and in African traditional religions: A theological critique", *Old Testament Essays* 8 (1995) 7–30.

————, "New data base: Bible in Africa research project", *Newsletter on African Old Testament Scholarship* 3 (1997) 3–4.

Kealy, S.P., "The canon: An African contribution", *Biblical Theology Bulletin* 9 (1979) 13–26.

Keita, S.O.Y., "Studies and comments on ancient Egyptian biological relationships", *History of Africa* 20 (1993) 129–154.

Kibicho, S.G., "The interaction of the traditional Kikuyu concept of God with the biblical concept", *Cahiers des Religions Africaines* 2 (1968) 223–238.

Kirk, G.S. & Raven, J.E., *The Presocratic Philosophers. A critical history with a selection of texts*. Cambridge: Cambridge University Press, 1971.

Knight, D.A. (ed.), *Ethics and politics in the Hebrew Bible*. Atlanta: Society of Biblical Literature, 1995 [= *Semeia* 66].

Kronholm, T., "Polygami och monogami i Gamla testamentet: Med en utblick över den antika judendomen och Nya testamentet", *Svensk Exegetisk Årsbok* 47 (1982) 48–92.

Laffey, A.L., *An introduction to the Old Testament: A feminist perspective*. Philadelphia: Fortress Press, 1988.

Lagerwerf, L., "African women doing theology: A survey", *Exchange* 19 (1990) 1–69.

Lang, B. (ed.), *Anthropological approaches to the Old Testament*. London: SPCK, 1985 (Issues in Religion and Theology; 8).

Lasebikan, G.L., *Prophecy or schizophrenia? A study of prophecy in the Old Testament and in selected Aladura churches*. Unpubl. diss. University of Ibadan, 1983.

————, "Prophets as political activists in the ancient Israelite monarchy", *Orita* 17/I (1985) 51–58.

————, "Sacrifice in the Old Testament", *Orita* 20/II (1988) 64–78.

Lategan, B.C., "Scholar and ordinary reader—more than a simple interface", *Semeia* 73 (1996) 255.

Lefkowitz, M.R. & MacLean Rogers, G. (eds.), *Black Athena revisited.* Chapel Hill: The University of North Carolina Press, 1996.

LeMarquand, G., "A bibliography of the Bible in Africa: A preliminary publication", *Bulletin for Contextual Theology* 2/II (1995) 6–40.

Little, K., *African women in towns: An aspect of Africa's social revolution.* Cambridge: Cambridge University Press, 1973.

Maag, V., *Text, Wortschatz und Begriffswelt des Buches Amos.* Leiden: Brill, 1951.

Mafico, T.L.J., "Parallels between Jewish and African religio-cultural lives", F. von Hammerstein (ed.), *Christian-Jewish relations in ecumenical perspective, with special emphasis on Africa.* Geneva: World Council of Churches (1978) 36–52.

————, *A study of the Hebrew root* שפט *with reference to Yahweh: A thesis.* Unpubl. diss. Harvard, 1979.

————, "The Old Testament and effective evangelism Africa", *International Review of Mission* 75 (1986) 400–409.

————, "The divine name Yahweh Elohim from an African perspective", F.F. Segovia & M.A. Tolbert (eds.), *Reading from this place. Volume II: Social location and biblical interpretation in global perspectives.* Minneapolis: Fortress Press (1995) 21–32.

————, "The divine compound name יהוה אלהים and Israel's monotheistic polytheism", *Journal of Northwest Semitic Languages* 22/I (1996) 155–173.

Maleme, T.-A., "Translating the locust invasion in the book of Joel into Kituba", *The Bible Translator* 36 (1985) 216–220.

Mann, P.S., "Toward a biblical understanding of polygamy", *Missiology* 17 (1989) 11–26.

Manus, C.U., "Elijah—a *nabi'* before the 'writing prophets': Some critical reflections", *African Journal of Biblical Studies* 1/I (1986) 25–34.

————, "The concept of death and the after-life in the Old Testament and Igbo traditional religion: Some reflections for contemporary missiology", *Mission Studies* 3/2 (1986) 41–56.

Marah, J.K., *Pan-African education: The last stage of educational developments in Africa*. Lewiston: The Edwin Mellen Press, 1989 (Studies in African Education; 2).

Martey, E., *African theology: Inculturation and liberation*. Maryknoll: Orbis Books, 1993.

Masenya, M.J., *Proverbs 31:10–31 in a South African context: A bosadi perspective*. Unpubl. diss. University of South Africa, 1996.

Mays, J.L., *Amos: A commentary*. Philadelphia: The Westminster Press, 1969.

Mbiti, J.S., "African Christians and Jewish religious heritage", F. von Hammerstein (ed.), *Christian-Jewish relations in ecumenical perspective, with special emphasis on Africa*. Geneva: World Council of Churches (1978) 13–19.

––––––, "The biblical basis in present trends of African theology", *Africa Theological Journal* 7/I (1978) 72–85.

––––––, *Bible and theology in African Christianity*. Nairobi: Oxford University Press, 1986.

McCray, W.A., *The black presence in the Bible: Discovering the black and African identity of Biblical persons and nations*. Chicago: Black Light Fellowship, 1990.

McKenzie, P., "The history of religions in Africa", M. Pye (ed.), *Marburg revisited: Institutions and strategies in the study of religion*. Marburg: Diagonal-Verlag (1989) 99–105.

Merker, M., *Die Masai: Ethnographische Monographie eines ostafrikanischen Semitenvolkes*. Berlin: Reimer, 1904.

Mijoga, H.B.P., "Some notes on the Septuagint translation of Isaiah 53", *Africa Theological Journal* 19/I (1990) 85–90.

––––––, "Hermeneutics in African instituted churches in Malawi", *Missionalia* 24 (1996) 358–371.

Miller, C.L., "Literary studies and African literature: The challenge of intercultural literacy", R.H. Bates & al. (eds.), *Africa and the disciplines. The contribution of research in Africa to the social sciences and humanities*. Chicago: University of Chicago Press (1993) 213–231.

Mojola, A.O., "Translating the term 'tribe' in the Bible—with special reference to African languages", *The Bible Translator* 40 (1989) 208–211.

——, "A 'female' god i East Africa: The problem of translating God's name among the Iraqw of Mbulu, Tanzania", *The Bible Translator* 46 (1995) 229–236.

——, "The 'tribes' of Israel? A Bible translator's dilemma", *Journal for the Study of the Old Testament* 81 (1998) 15–29.

Mondeh, D.E., "Sacrifice in Jewish and African traditions", F. von Hammerstein (ed.), *Christian-Jewish relations in ecumenical perspective, with special emphasis on Africa.* Geneva: World Council of Churches (1978) 76–81.

Monsengwo Pasinya, L., *La notion de 'nomos' dans le Pentateuque grec.* Rome: Biblical Institute Press, 1973 (Analecta Biblica; 52. Consociata cum Recherches Africaines de Théologie; 5).

——, "Le cadre littéraire de Genèse 1", *Biblica* 57 (1976) 225–241.

——, "Isaïe xix 16–25 et universalisme dans la LXX", J.A. Emerton (ed.), *Congress volume: Salamanca 1983.* Leiden: Brill (1985) 192–207 (Supplements to Vetus Testamentum; 36).

Moore, S.F., *Anthropology and Africa: Changing perspectives on a changing scene.* Charlottesville & London: The University Press of Virginia, 1994.

Mosala, I.J., *Biblical hermeneutics and black theology in South Africa.* Grand Rapids: Eerdmans, 1989.

Muutuki, J., "Library resources for Old Testament research in Nairobi", *Newsletter on African Old Testament Scholarship* 3 (1997) 5–7.

Mveng, E., "La bible et l'afrique noire", E. Mveng & R.Z. Werblowsky (eds.), *The Jerusalem congress on Black Africa and the Bible.* Jerusalem: Anti-Defamation League of B'nai B'rit (1972) 23–39.

——, *Les sources grecques de l'histoire négro-africaine depuis Homère jusqu'à Strabon.* Paris: Présence Africaine, 1972.

—— & Werblowsky, R. Zwi (eds.). *The Jerusalem congress on Black Africa and the Bible.* Jerusalem: Anti-Defamation League of B'nai B'rit, 1972.

Naré, L., *Proverbes salomoniens et proverbes mossi. Etude comparative à partir d'une nouvelle analyse de Pr 25–29*. Frankfurt a.m.: Peter Lang, 1986 (Europäische Hochschulschriften; xxiii/283).

Ndiokwere, N.I., *Prophecy and revolution: The role of prophets in the independent African churches and in biblical tradition*. London: S.P.C.K., 1981 [reworked Th.D. dissertation, Pont. Univ. Urbaniana, Rome, 1977].

Ndungu, N., "The Bible in an African independent church", H.W. Kinoti & J.M. Waliggo, *The Bible in African Christianity: Essays in Biblical theology*. Nairobi: Acton Publishers (1997) 58–67.

Newing, E.G., "A study of Old Testament curricula in Eastern and Central Africa", *Africa Theological Journal* 3/I (1970) 80–98.

Ngally, J., "Lecture africaine de la Bible et l'exégèse traditionelle", E. Mveng & R.J.Z. Werblowsky (eds.), *The Jerusalem congress on Black Africa and the Bible*. Jerusalem: Anti-Defamation League of B'nai B'rit (1972) 121–133.

North, R., "Ophir/Parvaim and Petra/Joktheel", *Proceedings of the World Congress of Jewish Studies* 4 (1967) 197–202.

Nthamburi, Z. & Waruta, D., "Biblical hermeneutics in African instituted churches", H.W. Kinoti & J.M. Waliggo (eds.), *The Bible in African Christianity: Essays in Biblical Theology*. Nairobi: Acton Publishers (1997) 40–57.

Ntreh, B.A., *Transmission of political authority in ancient Israel: A tradition historical study of the demise and succession of kings in the Deuteronomistic history and in the Chronicler's history*. Unpubl. diss. Lutheran School of Theology, Chicago, 1989.

———, "Toward an African biblical hermeneutical [sic]", *Africa Theological Journal* 19 (1990) 247–254.

Nyeme Tese, J., "Continuite et discontinuite entre l'ancien testament et les religions africain", D. Atal Sa Angang (ed.), *Christianisme et identité africaine. Point de vue exegetique: Actes du 1er congres des biblistes africains*. Kinshasa: Faculte de theologie catholique, (1980) 83–112.

Nzambi, P.D., *Proverbes bibliques et proverbes kongo*. Frankfurt a.M.: Peter Lang, 1992 (Religionswissenschaft; 5).

Obbo, C., *African women: Their struggle for economic independence.* London: Zed Press, 1980.

Obijole, O.O., "The age of Agrican [sic] biblical theology has dawned", *Orita* 18/I (1986) 53–55.

O'Connor, D., *Ancient Nubiah: Egypt's Rival in Africa.* Philadelphia: University of Pennsylvania, 1993.

Oduyoye, M., "The spider, the chameleon and the creation of the earth", E.A.A. Adegbola (ed.), *Traditional religion in West Africa.* Ibadan: Daystar Press (1983) 374–388.

————, *The sons of the gods and the daughters of men: An Afro-Asiatic interpretation of Genesis 1–11.* Maryknoll: Orbis Books & Ibadan: Daystar Press, 1984.

Oduyoye, M.A., "Naming the woman: The words of the Akan and the words of the Bible", *Bulletin of African Theology* 3 (1985) 81–97.

————, *Hearing and knowing. Theological reflections on Christianity in Africa.* Maryknoll: Orbis Books, 1986.

Okeke, G.E., "Concepts of future life: Biblical and Igbo", *Neue Zeitschrift für Missionswissenschaft* 44 (1988) 178–196.

Okwueze, M.R., *Myth: The Old Testament experience.* Unpubl. diss. University of Nigeria, 1995.

Olubunmo, D.A., "Israelite concept of ideal king: A model of interdependence of politics and religion for Nigeria", *African Journal of Biblical Studies* 6/II (1991) 59–67.

Onah, A.O., "Prophet Ezekiel's concept of individuality: Guidelines for Nigeria", *African Journal of Biblical Studies* 6/II (1991) 68–78.

Onaiyekan, J., *The priesthood in pre-monarchial ancient Israel and among the Owe-Yoruba of Kabba: A comparative study.* Unpubl. diss. Pontificia Universitas Urbaniana, Rome, 1976.

Onibere, S.G.A., "Old Testament sacrifice in African tradition: A case of scapegoatism", M. Augustin & K.-D. Schunk (eds.), *'Wünschet Jerusalem Frieden': Collected communications to the XIIth congress of the International Organization for the Study of the Old Testament, Jerusalem 1986.* Frankfurt a.M.: Peter Lang (1988) 193–203 (Beiträge zur Erforschung des Alten Testaments und des Antiken Judentums; 13).

Onwu, N., "The current state of biblical studies in Africa", *Journal of Religious Thought* 41 (1985) 35–46.

Onwurah, E., "Isaiah 14: Its bearing on African life and thought", *Bible Bhashyam* 13 (1987) 29–41.

Oosthuizen, G.C., "Hebraïes-judaïstiese trekke in die onafhanklike kerke (OK) en religieuse bewegings op die swart bevolkung in Suid-Afrika", *Nederduitse Gereformeerde Teologiese Tydskrif* 30 (1989) 333–345.

Oosthuizen, R. de W., "African experience of time and its compatibility with the Old Testament view of time as suggested in the genealogy of Genesis 5", *Old Testament Essays* 6 (1993) 190–204.

Osuji, B.A., *The Hebrew and Igbo concept of religion and sin compared in the light of biblical and rabbinic material.* Unpubl. diss. Pontificia Universitas Urbaniana, Rome, 1967.

Otto, E., *Theologisches Ethik des Alten Testaments.* Stuttgart: W. Kohlhammer, 1994 (Theologische Wissenschaft; 3.2).

Overholt, T.W., *Prophecy in a cross-cultural perspective.* Atlanta: Scholars Press, 1986.

———, *Cultural anthropology and the Old Testament.* Minneapolis: Fortress, 1996 (Guides to Biblical Scholarship, OT series).

Owan, K., "The fundamentalist's interpretation of the Bible: A challenge to biblical exegetes in West Africa", *West African Journal of Ecclesial Studies* 5 (1993) 1–15.

Parkin, D. & Nyamwaya, D. (eds.), *Transformations of African marriage.* Manchester: Manchester University Press, 1987 (International African Seminars New Series; 3).

Pauw, C.M., "Theological education in Africa", *Old Testament Essays* 7 (1994) 13–24.

Pfeifer, G., *Ägypten im Alten Testament.* München: Biblische Notizen, 1995 (Biblische Notizen Beihefte; 8).

Platvoet, J., "The institutional environment of the study of religions in Africa south of the Sahara", M. Pye (ed.), *Marburg revisited: Institutions and strategies in the study of religion.* Marburg: Diagonal-Verlag (1989) 107–126.

Pobee, J.S., "The use of the Bible in African theology", T. Fornberg (ed.), *Bible, hermeneutics, mission*. Uppsala: Swedish Institute for Missionary Research (1995) 113–130 (Missio; 10).

Punt, J., "Reading the Bible in Africa: Accounting for some trends (Part I)", *Scriptura* 68 (1999) 1–11.

Radcliffe-Brown, A.R. & Forde, D. (eds.), *African systems of kinship and marriage*. Oxford: Oxford University Press, 1950.

Redford, D.B., "Kush", *The Anchor Bible Dictionary* 4 (1992) 109–111.

Renju, P.M., "African traditional religions & Old Testament: Continuity or discontinuity", D. Atal Sa Angang (ed.), *Christianisme et identité africaine. Point de vue exegetique: Actes du 1er congres des biblistes africains*. Kinshasa: Faculte de theologie catholique (1980) 113–118.

Rice, G., "Was Amos a racist?", *Journal of Religious Thought* 35 (1978) 35–44.

——, "The African roots of the prophet Zephaniah", *Journal of Religious Thought* 36 (1979) 21–31.

Riches, J., "Interpreting the Bible in African contexts: Glasgow consultation", *Ministerial Formation* 67 (1994) 58–59.

——, "Interpreting the Bible in African contexts: Glasgow consultation", *Semeia* 73 (1996) 181–188.

Rogers, R.G., "Biblical hermeneutics and contemporary African theology", L.M. Hopfe (ed.), *Uncovering ancient stones: Essays in memory of H. Neil Richardson*. Wiona Lake: Eisenbrauns (1994) 245–260.

Rogerson, J., *Anthropology and the Old Testament*. Oxford: Blackwell, 1978.

——, *Genesis 1–11*. Sheffield: JSOT Press, 1991 (Old Testament Guides).

—— & al. (eds.), *The Bible in ethics: The second Sheffield colloquium*. Sheffield: Sheffield Academic Press, 1995 (Journal for the Study of the Old Testament Supplement Series; 207).

Ross, K.R., "What has Jerusalem to do with Athens? Theology at the University of Malawi", *Ministerial Formation* 56 (1992) 3–6.

le Roux, J.H., *A story of two ways: Thirty years of Old Testament scholarship in South Africa.* Pretoria: Verba Vitae, 1993 (Old Testament Essays Supplement Series; 2).

Rwehumbiza, P., *A comparative study between the development of Yahwistic monotheism and the concept of God among the Bantu people south of the Sahara: A biblico-theological evaluation.* Partly publ. diss. Pontificia Universitas Laterana, Rome, 1983.

————, *Patriarchal and Bantu cults compared.* Eldoret: Amecea Gaba Publications, 1988 (Spearhead Series; 103).

Saint, W.S., *Universities in Africa: Strategies for stabilization and revitalization.* Washington D.C.: The World Bank, 1992 (World Bank Technical Paper; 194).

Sarna, N.M., *Genesis.* Philadelphia: Jewish Publication Society, 1989 (The Jewish Publication Society Torah Commentary).

Scullion, J.J., *Genesis: A commentary for students, teachers, and preachers.* Collegeville: Liturgical Press, 1992 (Old Testament Studies; 6).

Sempore, S., "Le noir et le salut dans la bible", P. Adeso & al. (eds.), *Universalisme et mission dans la bible: Actes du cinquième congrès des biblistes africains.* Nairobi: Catholic Biblical Centre for Africa and Madagascar (1993) 17–29.

Simbandumwe, S.S., *A socio-religious and political analysis of the Judeo-Christian concept of prophetism and modern Bakongo and Zulu African prophet movements.* Lewiston, New York: Edwin Mellen Press, 1992 (African Studies; 28).

Simons, J., *The geographical and topographical texts of the Old Testament.* Leiden: Brill, 1959.

Smith, H.P., *A critical and exegetical commentary on the Books of Samuel.* Edinburgh: T. & T. Clark, 1898 (The International Critical Commentary).

Smith, R., "A new perspective on Amos 9:7a: 'To me, O Israel, you are just like the Kushites'", *Journal of the Interdenominational Centre* 22 (1994) 36–47.

Snowden Jr., F.M., *Blacks in antiquity: Ethiopians in the Greco-Roman experience.* Cambridge, Massachusetts: Belknap Press, 1970.

Snyman, G.F., "'Ilahle Elinothuthu'? The lay reader and/or the critical reader—some remarks on africanisation", *Religion & Theology* 6 (1999) 140–167.

Soggin, J.A., *The Prophet Amos: A translation and commentary.* London: SCM, 1987.

Stassen, S.L., "Die rol van Egipte, Kus en Seba in Jesaja 43:3 en 45:14", *Journal for Semitics* 4 (1992) 160–180.

Sugirtharajah, R.S. (ed.), *The Postcolonial Bible.* Sheffield: Sheffield Academic Press, 1998 (The Bible and Postcolonialism; 1).

Swanepoel, M.G., "An encounter between Old Testament theology and African concepts of God", *Theologia Viatorum* 18 (1990) 20–30.

Tesfai, Y., *This is my resting place: An inquiery into the role of time and space in the Old Testament.* Unpubl. diss. Lutheran School of Theology, Chicago, 1975.

Thompson, J.A., "Bible geographies and atlases and their use in translating", *The Bible Translator* 32 (1981) 431–437.

Török, L., *The Kingdom of Kush: Handbook of the Napatan-Meroitic Civilization.* Leiden etc.: Brill, 1997 (Handbuch der Orientalistik; 1/31).

Trigger, B.G., *Nubia under the Pharaohs.* London: Thames & Hudson, 1976.

Trobisch, W., *My wife made me a polygamist.* Kehl/Rhein: Editions Trobisch, 1967.

Turner, H., *Profile through preaching.* London: World Council of Churches, Commission on world mission and evangelism, 1965; repr.: Birmingham: Selly Oak Colleges, 1984 (The Study Centre for New Religious Movements. Monograph Series; 1).

Tutu, D., "Some African insights and the Old Testament", *Journal of Theology for Southern Africa* 1 (1972) 16–22.

——, "Survey of theological institutions in Africa today", *All-Africa Conference of Churches Bulletin* 9/II (1976) 7–27.

Ugwueze, O.F., *Igbo proverbs and biblical proverbs.* Unpubl. diss. Pontificia Universitas Urbaniana, Rome, 1976.

Ukpong, J.S., *Sacrifice: African and biblical: A comparative study of Ibibo and levitical sacrifices*. Rome: Urbaniana University Press, 1987.

————, "Rereading the Bible with African eyes", *Journal of Theology for Southern Africa* 91 (1995) 3–14.

————, "Popular readings of the Bible in Africa and implications for academic readings: Report from the field research carried out on oral interpretation of the Bible in Port Harcourt Metropolis, Nigeria under the auspices of the Bible in Africa Project, 1991–94", forthcoming in G. West & M.W. Dube (eds.), *The Bible in Africa*. Leiden: Brill, 2000.

Ullendorff, E., *Ethiopia and the Bible*. Oxford: Oxford University Press, 1968 (The Schweich lectures).

de Vaux, R., *Ancient Israel: Its life and institutions*. London: Darton, Longman & Todd, [1965^2] 1984.

de Waard, J. & Smalley, W.A., *A translator's handbook on the Book of Amos*. New York: United Bible Societies 1979.

Wambutda, D.N., "Hermeneutics and the search for theologia africana", *Africa Theological Journal* 9/I (1980) 29–39.

————, "Hebrewisms of West Africa: An ongoing search in the correlations between the Old Testament and African Weltanschauung", *Ogbomoso Journal of Theology* 2 (1987) 33–41.

Weber, H.R., *The Book that reads me: A handbook for Bible study enablers*. Geneva: World Council of Churches Publications, 1995.

Wenham, G.J., *Genesis 1–15*. Dallas: Word Incorporated, 1987 (Word Biblical Commentary; 1).

West, G.O., *Contextual Bible study*. Pietermaritzburg: Cluster Publications, 1993.

————, "Difference and dialogue: Reading the Joseph story with poor and marginalized communities in South Africa", *Biblical Interpretation* 2 (1994) 152–170.

————, *Biblical hermeneutics of liberation: Modes of reading the Bible in the South African context*. Pietermaritzburg: Cluster Publications, 1995^2.

————, "Reading the Bible differently: Giving shape to the discourse of the dominated", *Semeia* 73 (1996) 21–41.

————, "On the eve of an African biblical studies: Trajectories and trends", *Journal of Theology for Southern Africa* 99 (1997) 99–115.

————, "Early encounters with the Bible in Africa: Historical, methodological, and hermeneutical analysis of the transactions between the Bible and indigenous African communities", *Newsletter on African Old Testament Scholarship* 6 (1999) 16–18.

Westermann, C., *Genesis 1–11*. Neukirchen-Vluyn: Neukirchener Verlag, 1974 (Biblischer Kommentar Altes Testament; I/1).

Williams, J.J., *Hebrewisms of West Africa: From Nile to Niger with the Jews*. London, 1930; repr. New York: Biblo & Tannen, 1967.

Williams, R.J., "II. Ägypten und Israel", *Theologische Realenzyklopädie* 1 (1977) 492–505.

Yorke, G.L., "Biblical hermeneutics: An Afrocentric perspective", *Religion and Theology* 2 (1995) 145–158.

Young III, J.U., "African theology: From independence to liberation", *Voices from the third world* 10/IV (1987) 41–48.

————, *African theology: A critical analysis and annotated bibliography*. Westport: Greenwood Press, 1993 (Bibliographies and indexes in religious studies; 26).

Zinkuratire, V., *The kingship of Yahweh in Israel's history, cult and eschatology: A study of Psalm 47*. Unpubl. diss. University of Cambridge, 1987.

————, "The African Bible project", *Newsletter on African Old Testament Scholarship* 4 (1998) 7–9.

van Zyl, D.C., "In Africa theology is not thought out but danced out: On the theological significance of Old Testament symbolism and rituals in African Zionist churches", *Old Testament Essays* 8 (1995) 425–438.

————, "Interpretasie van die Ou Testament in Sionistiese kerke—'n verkennende studie", *Nederduitse Gereformeerde Teologiese Tydskrif* 38 (1997) 85–93.

Index of Authors

A

Abe, G.O.: 16, 17, 19, 20, 33, 44, 62–75, 87, 88

Abegunde, S.O.: 19

Abogunrin, S.O.: 11, 16, 21, 22, 38, 39, 46, 56, 58, 69

Abotchie, F.F.K.: 13, 14

Adamo, D.T.: 20, 25, 32, 44, 48, 54, 56, 95, 97, 100, 101, 102, 103, 112–114, 116

Adams, W.: 99, 108

de Adegbola, E.A.A.: 31

Adelowo, E.D.: 32, 69

Ademiluka, S.: 54

Adutwum, O.: 19, 20

Ajayi, J.F. Ade: 11, 45

Akao, J.O.: 21

Akpunonu, P.D.: 12

Alao, D.: 21

Anderson, F.I.: 117

Anderson, R.W.: 95, 100, 102, 103, 124

Assimeng, M.: 41

Atal Sa Angang, D.: 14

Atteh, S.O.: 47

B

Bach, A.: 117

Bailey, R.C.: 24, 94, 103

Bajeux, J.-C.: 10, 30

Barret, D.B.: 41, 78

Bates, M.S.: 10

Bediaku, B.J.B.: 13

Bennett, R.A.: 95, 97, 124

Bernal, M.: 117

Blum, W.G.: 86

Boulaga, F.E.: 69, 72

Bowen, D.N.: 25, 49, 56

Bowers, P.: 28, 45

Bratcher, R.G.: 111
Burden, J.J.: 24, 30, 40
Bürkle, H.: 53

C
Caird, G.B.: 118
Carter, C.E.: 86
Clignet, R.: 80
Cogan, M.: 98
Copher, C.B.: 97, 124
Conradie, E.M.: 59
Currid, J.D.: 97

D
Deist, F.E.: 24, 27, 40, 46, 57, 59, 75
Dickson, K.A.: 12, 14, 15, 29, 31, 32,
    36, 42, 69
Djitangar, E.E.: 21
Domatob, J.K.: 45
Donaldson, L.E.: 118
Draper, J.A.: 59
Dubois, M.J.: 37

E
Ebo, D.J.I.: 16, 20, 21
Ehret, C.: 97
Ehrlich, A.B.: 119
Ekpo, M.U.: 21
Ela, J.-M.: 33, 72, 74
Engelken, K.: 81
Enomate, J.M.: 21
Eribo, F.: 44
Etuk, E.S.: 47
Evans-Pritchard, E.E.: 43, 79, 86, 87
Even-Shoshan, A.: 96

F
Fasholé-Luke, E.E.: 18
Felder, C.H.: 106
Fiedler, K.: 22, 44
Fiensy, D.: 39, 87
Flint, P.W.: 40
Forde, D.: 79
Forslund, E.: 53
Fortes, M.: 79
Freedman, D.N.: 117

G
Gakindi, G.: 16, 20
Gese, H.: 102, 121
Gitau, S.: 16, 19, 60
Goba, B.: 13
Golka, F.W.: 35, 39
Görg, M.: 104
Gowan, D.E.: 35

H
Haak, R.H.: 100
Habtu, T.: 20
Hamilton, V.P.: 81
Hammershaimb, E.: 116
von Hammerstein, F.: 14
Harper, W.R.: 102, 115, 116
Hays, J.D.: 100, 101, 103, 106, 124
Hidal, S.: 100, 124
Hillman, E.: 78, 86
Hinga, T.M.: 57
Holter, K.: 10, 19, 20, 23, 25, 43, 48,
    55, 56, 57, 58, 100, 105, 116, 118
Høyland, M.: 20, 95, 116

I
Idowu, E.B.: 12, 14

Ifesieh, E.I.: 88
Ita, M.: 65

J
Jackson, A.A.: 95
Jonker, L.C.: 59

K
Kalugila, L.: 17, 20
Kanyoro, M.R.A.: 84, 85, 89
Kawale, W.R.: 18, 25, 36, 37, 56
Kealy, S.P.: 94
Keita, S.O.Y.: 96
Kibicho, S.G.: 13
Kirk, G.S.: 110
Knight, D.A.: 38
Kronholm, T.: 81

L
Laffey, A.L.: 81
Lagerwerf, L.: 89
Lang, B.: 86
Lasebikan, G.L.: 16, 19, 20, 21
Lategan, B.C.: 59
Lefkowitz, M.R.: 117
LeMarquand, G.: 19, 43, 55
Little, K.: 80

M
Maag, V.: 119
MacLean Rogers, G.: 117
Mafico, T.L.J.: 12, 14, 19
Maleme, T.-A.: 32
Mann, P.S.: 83, 84, 87, 88, 89
Manus, C.U.: 33, 58, 62–75
Marah, J.K.: 10
Martey, E.: 88

Masenya, M.J.: 19
Mays, J.L.: 116
Mbiti, J.S.: 12, 14, 17, 18, 20, 22, 42, 52, 56
McCray, W.A.: 117
McKenzie, P.: 46
Merker, M.: 30
Meyers, C.L.: 86
Mijoga, H.B.P.: 21, 42, 53
Miller, C.L.: 39
Mojola, A.O.: 19, 34
Mondeh, D.E.: 13
Monsengwo Pasinya, L.: 12, 21
Moore, S.F.: 79
Mosala, I.J.: 24, 32, 73
Muutuki, J.: 25, 49, 56
Mveng, E.: 13, 14, 72, 95, 97, 117

N
Naré, L.: 17, 19, 35
Ndiokwere, N.I.: 12, 33
Ndungu, N.: 42, 54
Newing, E.G.: 11
Ngally, J.: 36
North, R.: 95
Nthamburi, Z.: 42
Ntreh, B.A.: 18, 20, 37
Nyamwaya, D.: 80
Nyeme Tese, J.: 30
Nzambi, P.D.: 17, 19

O
Obbo, C.: 79
Obijole, O.O.: 17
O'Connor, D.: 100, 124
Oduyoye, M.: 17, 31, 32, 35
Oduyoye, M.A.: 33, 72, 74, 89

Okeke, G.E.: 32, 69
Okwueze, M.R.: 20
Olubunmo, D.A.: 34, 62
Onah, A.O.: 62
Onaiyekan, J.: 13
Onibere, S.G.A.: 19, 32
Onwu, N.: 38, 46, 56, 58
Onwurah, E.: 30
Oosthuizen, G.C.: 42, 54
Oosthuizen, R. de W.: 30
Osuji, B.A.: 12
Otto, E.: 38
Overholt, T.W.: 86, 87
Owan, K.: 59

P
Parkin, D.: 80
Pauw, C.M.: 28, 45
Pfeifer, G.: 97
Platvoet, J.: 11, 44
Pobee, J.S.: 75
Punt, J.: 56

R
Radcliffe-Brown, A.R.: 79
Raven, J.E.: 110
Redford, D.B.: 108, 124
Renju, P.M.: 15
Reyburn, W.D.: 111
Rice, G.: 103, 116, 117
Riches, J.: 53, 75
Rogers, R.G.: 56, 74
Rogerson, J.: 35, 38, 86
Ross, K.R.: 44
le Roux, J.H.: 24, 27, 39, 40, 41
Rwehumbiza, P.: 19, 32

S
Saint, W.S.: 50
Sarna, N.M.: 35
Scullion, J.J.: 35
Sempore, S.: 97, 116
Simbandumwe, S.S.: 17
Simons, J.: 104, 124
Smalley, W.A.: 111, 116
Smith, H.P.: 102, 118
Smith, R.: 102, 116, 117, 119
Snowden Jr., F.M.: 110
Snyman, G.F.: 59
Soggin, J.A.: 117
Stassen, S.L.: 103
Sugirtharajah, R.S.: 118
Swanepoel, M.G.: 24, 40

T
Tesfai, Y.: 12
Thompson, J.A.: 107, 112
Török, L.: 124
Trigger, B.G.: 99, 108
Trobisch, W.: 77
Turner, H.: 53
Tutu, D.: 11, 82, 83, 87

U
Ugwueze, O.F.: 13
Ukpong, J.S.: 16, 18, 19, 36, 37, 46, 53, 55
Ullendorff, E.: 101, 116

V
de Vaux, R.: 81

W
de Waard, J.: 111, 116

Wambutda, D.N.: 15, 21, 31, 45
Waruta, D.: 42
Weber, H.R.: 51
Wenham, G.J.: 35
West, G.O.: 24, 32, 37, 43, 52, 54, 56,
    59, 73
Westermann, C.: 101
Williams, J.J.: 15, 30, 31
Williams, R.J.: 97

Y
Yorke, G.L.: 46, 94, 106
Young III, J.U.: 55, 62, 72–73

Z
Zinkuratire, V.: 18, 20
van Zyl, D.C.: 42, 54

Index of Subjects

A

African Instituted Churches: 14, 41, 54–55

African presence in the OT: 19–20, 93–106, 107–114, 115–125

African theology: 12, 14, 42, 88

Africanisation: 45, 47

Afrocentrism: 106

Anglophone Africa: 16, 44

article: 17, 19, 20, 23

arts: 54

B

bibliography: 55

Burkina Faso: 17, 35

C

Cameroon: 16

canon: 94

cartography: 94–95

Central African Republic: 16, 45

church life: 28–29, 52–55

commentary: 17–18, 23, 31, 35

comparison, religio-cultural: 13–14, 18–19, 29, 39, 50, 82–89

comparison, socio-cultural: 29, 32–34, 39, 45, 50, 63–65

conference: 1–5, 13, 14, 27, 34, 41, 51, 61, 77

Congo [& Zaïre]: 14, 17, 19, 21, 28

context, institutional: 3, 9–25, 35–38, 41–50, 55–57, 57–60

context, popular: 3, 52–55

context, traditional: 21, 30, 43

contextualisation: 22, 45–47

covenant: 20, 62–71

creation: 32

curriculum: 11–12, 60

Cush: 4, 99–104, 107–114, 115–125

D

de-Africanisation: 94
doctoral dissertation: 13, 17, 18, 19

E

economic resources: 35–38, 47–50
education policy: 44–47
Egypt: 96–99
Ethiopia: 20, 110–111
Eurocentrism: 105–106
exegesis: 20–22, 46

F

Francophone Africa: 16, 44
funding: 47–50

G

Ghana: 12, 13, 18, 19, 20, 28

H

hermeneutics: 1, 37, 71–76, 105–106,
    113–114
hermeneutics, inculturation: 18, 24, 29–
    32, 37–38, 88–89
hermeneutics, liberation: 24, 32, 89
humanities: 45

I

independence: 10, 117
infrastructure: 47–50, 56
interaction, academic and popular: 57–
    60
interaction, African and Western: 34–
    38, 38–40, 48
interpretation history: 115–118

J

journal: 13, 17, 21, 23, 28, 35, 47

K

Kenya: 12, 16, 19, 28, 45, 49

L

library: 48–50, 56

M

Madagascar: 55
Malawi: 18, 21
marginalisation: 34–38
methodology: 15, 18, 31, 36–38, 46–
    47, 66–71, 85–89
mythology: 20

N

Nigeria: 3, 4, 12, 13, 16, 17, 18, 19, 20,
    21, 24, 44, 45, 49, 61–76, 116
North Africa: 9

O

organisations: 14, 18

P

polygamy: 77–90
post-graduate studies, Africa: 16, 22
post-graduate studies, the West: 12,
    15–16
predilection for the OT: 42
prophetism: 19, 21, 33, 62–71
proverbs: 13, 17, 19, 35, 39
publishing: 17, 23

R

relevance: 38–39, 46
research history: 9–25, 29–34, 55–56
research policy: 3, 5, 44–47, 58
research situation: 51–60
rites of passage: 32

rituals: 54
Rwanda: 20

S
sacrifice: 13, 19, 32
seminary: 2, 9–25, 28, 45
Septuagint: 21, 107–108, 110
sermon: 53
Sierra Leone: 18
social anthropology: 78–80
social criticism: 61–76
South Africa: 13, 24, 30, 39–40

T
Tanzania: 13, 17, 24, 28
Tchad: 21
technological development: 24–25
textbook: 23
Togo: 13
translation: 4, 19, 107–114

U
university: 2, 9–25, 28, 44, 49, 60

W
Western guild: 1, 16, 28, 94–95, 115–117
world-view: 14, 29, 43

Z
Zimbabwe: 95

Index of Biblical References

Pentateuch	12	26:34	81
		28:8–9	83
Genesis		28:9	81
1–11	17, 31, 35	29:15–30	81
2–3	81, 100	37–50	37
2:10–14	100, 101, 113	41:41–57	98
2:13	100, 101, 113,		
	122	Exodus	73
2:24	88	1–11	97
4:19–22	83	1:5–7	98
10	104	2:21–22	101
10:6	101, 104, 113,	12–14	97
	122	13:3	97
10:7	101, 104, 122	16:2	98
10:8	101, 122	20:2	98
10:14	104	20:17	81
13:10	98	21:7–11	81
16:1 ff.	81	21:10	84, 89
26:2	98		

Leviticus

    24:10–16   98

Numbers

    11:5   98

    12:1   101, 122

Deuteronomy

    4:20   97

    5:6   98

    5:15   97

    17:17   81, 89

    21:15–17   81, 84

    23:4–9   98

    26:5–10   97

Joshua

    24:5   98

Judges

    8:30   81

    10:4   81

    12:8–9   81

    19:1   81

1 Samuel

    1:2   81

    10:18   98

    25:1–44   81

2 Samuel

    3:2–5   81

    5:13   81

    12:8   83

    18:21–32   102, 109, 122

1 Kings

    10   105

    11:3   81

    11:40   98

    19   33, 64, 65

    22:49   104

2 Kings

    18:21.24   98

    19:9 ff.   102, 109, 122

    25:26   98

1 Chronicles

    1   104

    1:8   122

    1:9   104, 122

    1:10   122

2 Chronicles

    6:5   99

    7:22   99

    9   105

    12:2–4   103

    12:3   122

    13:21   83

    14:8–14   103, 113, 122, 123

    16:8   103, 104

    21:16   122

    24:2–3   84

Ezra   21

Esther

    1:1   104, 109, 122

    8:9   122

Nehemiah

    9:9 ff.   99

Job

    28:16   104

    28:19   104, 122

Psalms

    7:1   122

    47   20, 54, 55

    68:32   99, 104, 111, 122, 123

    72:10.15   105

    81:6.11   99

    87:4   104, 122, 123

    105:23.38   99

    114:1   99

    135:8–9   99

    136:10   99

Proverbs   13, 17, 19, 35

    12:4   81

    18:22   81

    31:10–31   19

Isaiah

    11:11   104, 109, 122

    13:12   104

    14   30

    18   103, 123

    18:1   122

    18:2   103, 109

    18:7   103

    19:16–25   12, 21

    19:25   99

    20   99, 103, 109, 122

    30:1–5   99

    31:1–3   99

    37:9   122

    40–55   12

    43:3   103, 105, 109, 122

    45:14   103, 109, 122

    45:15   105

    53   21

Jeremiah

    2:18   101

    13:23   103, 109, 115, 122

    36:14   122

    38–39   102, 122

    44:1   104

    44:14   104

    44:15   104

    46:2–12   99

    46:8–9   104

    46:9   104, 122

    46:14–28   99

Ezekiel   62

    27:22–23   105

    29   99

    29:10   99, 109, 111, 122

    29:14   104

    30   99

    30:4–5   104, 122

    30:5   104

    30:9   122

    31   99

    38:5   102, 122

Daniel

    9:15   99

11:43   102

Joel   32

Amos   20, 115–125
    1:3–2:16   121
    1:6–8   121
    2:4–5   121
    2:6–16   121
    3:2   121
    3:3–5   119
    4:13   121
    5:8–9   121
    9:5–6   121
    9:7   4, 102, 111, 113,
               115–125
    9:7–15   121

Nahum
    3:9   102, 104

Zephaniah
    1:1   103, 113, 122
    2:4–15   103, 109
    2:12   103, 109, 113,
               122
    3:10   103, 113, 122

Ben Sira
    24:27   101

Bible & Theology in Africa

The twentieth century made sub-Saharan Africa a Christian continent. This formidable church growth is reflected in a wide range of attempts at contextualizing Christian theology and biblical interpretation in Africa. At a grassroots level ordinary Christians express their faith and read the bible in ways reflecting their daily situation; at an academic level, theologians and biblical scholars relate the historical traditions and sources of Christianity to the socio- and religio-cultural context of Africa. In response to this, the Bible and Theology in Africa series aims at making African theology and biblical interpretation its subject as well as object, as the concerns of African theologians and biblical interpreters will be voiced and critically analyzed. Both Africans and Western authors are encouraged to consider this series.

Inquiries and manuscripts should be directed to:

Dr. Knut Holter
Associate Professor of Old Testament
Misjonsvegen 34
N-4024 Stavanger
Norway